—— THE ——
LOS ANGELES
REVIEW

THE
LOS ANGELES
REVIEW

VOLUME 19 • SPRING 2016

EDITOR • KATE GALE
MANAGING EDITOR • ALISA TRAGER
ASSISTANT MANAGING EDITOR • CARLY JOY MILLER
ASSISTANT MANAGING EDITOR • REBECCA BAUMANN

FICTION EDITOR • SEAN BERNARD
POETRY EDITOR • MAGGIE HESS / BLAS FALCONER
ASSISTANT POETRY EDITOR • TALIA SHALEV
POETRY ASSISTANT • S.H. LOHMANN
NONFICTION EDITOR • ANN BEMAN
BOOK REVIEWS EDITOR • ALYSE BENSEL
ASSISTANT BOOK REVIEWS EDITOR • DANIEL PECCHENINO
DESIGNER • SELENA TRAGER

THE LOS ANGELES REVIEW IS A PUBLICATION OF RED HEN PRESS

The Los Angeles Review (ISSN 1543-3536) is published by Red Hen Press.
Copyright © 2016 by Red Hen Press

The Los Angeles Review is published twice yearly. The editors welcome electronic submissions of fiction, nonfiction, poetry, book reviews, profiles, and interviews. Please go to www.losangelesreview.org for guidelines and reading periods. All rights revert to author on publication.

Subscription rates for individuals: US $20.00 per year. Libraries and institutions: $24.00 per year. Subscriptions outside the US add $10.00 per year for air mail. Classroom and bookstore discounts available. Remittance to be made by money order or by a check drawn on a US bank.

Visit us online at www.losangelesreview.org.

Cover image: *Surveillance* by Jamie Clifford

ISBN: 978-1-59709-420-7

Acknowledgments: The works and ideas published in *The Los Angeles Review* belong to the individuals to whom such works and ideas are attributed, and do not necessarily represent or express the opinions of Red Hen Press, any of its advisors or other individuals associated with the publication of this journal. Certain works herein have been previously published and are reprinted by permission of the author and/or publisher.

The Ahmanson Foundation, the National Endowment for the Arts, The Los Angeles County Arts Commission, the Los Angeles Department of Cultural Affairs, the Dwight Stuart Youth Fund, the Pasadena Arts & Culture Commission and the City of Pasadena Cultural Affairs Division, and Sony Pictures Entertainment partially support Red Hen Press.

CONTENTS

NONFICTION

REVIEWS

TO OUR READERS

KATE GALE

WELCOME TO THE new *Los Angeles Review*. We are pleased to welcome our new poetry editor, Blas Falconer, who is apt to shake things up a bit. He writes in "To Orpheus,"

> ... Tonight,
>
> you're the swan, lost among pinholes of light,
> your throat bitten by a black hole

And just like that, his poetry, voice, ideas and generous spirit make us feel that we are swans rising into the black air. Rising above the impossible into the possible. That's what story, poetry and the world of imagination should do, chill the backs of our necks and make us feel like we are in some dark, wild place where the world was created. Literature isn't supposed to be comforting, it's supposed to surprise, alarm, awaken—and these stories, poems and flashes of story do just that.

You won't feel like sitting around after you read them. You'll feel like walking, singing, dancing; you'll feel like thinking, about how the people in the world you live in ache, and love, sleep and wake into a place that is wilder than you'd ever imagined.

CIRCUS SONNET

ADRIENNE CHRISTIAN

for emmanuel

manny, let's instead of

letting the rents

sacrifice us,

kill ourselves. we should do it.

at the hour when the men come

to have us,

we could already be gone.

we could even use their own weapons

to do it. my mother's ropes.

your daddy's trees. I know a place.

i know you're tired of this yoke.

think of the egg on their prick faces—

every stadium seat filled, but no performers.

let them sacrifice their own bodies, those fuckers.

EDITORS' CHOICE
KATE GALE

LOVEMAKIN WHEN YOU TRYNA GET A BOOK DEAL

Adrienne Christian

for tayari j. and sandra a.

i love this poet turned publisher.
but i can't slide down on his wood and ride
because two ladies told me
don't.
when you are sitting at the table
let no soul say
you screwed yourself
into that position.
hear me, girl.

i am not at that table yet.
so we grind.
he kisses me. he kisses mine.
i tell him
stop. we grind. he holds
me. he hugs me. he's
hung. he touches me where i tell him
noplease quitit or i'mma hafta leave
if you don't quitit we grind.
he won't let me leave,

takes my purse. he says please i say
pleasestop. and it's just so sad, ya know?—
a grown man beggin me to do what's
fair.
we grind. he

sits me on his lap and i can hardly
keep my face from it. but i must and i will till
i get myself at least two books
say the ladies, and they know because
they're already where i'm tryna go.
so we grind. his blue top sheet and the ladies' words
the only things keeping us from love.

and i write.
he's got a million books
he lends me.
i write a hundred poems
i send him.
he wants me at important parties
but i won't be seen out with this man.
he gives me feedback on my work.
he wants me at the table. he wants me.
i want him
but i want books
more.

ORLANDO AWARDS

INSPIRED BY THE life and work of Virginia Woolf, the A Room of Her Own Foundation (AROHO) is a nonprofit organization that connects, challenges, and champions women writers. AROHO's Fall 2015 Orlando Award winners are published in this issue of *The Los Angeles Review*.

ORLANDO

GROW HEAVY

LEIGH CLAIRE SCHMIDLI

"Subtle, tender, poignant, this story delivers an emotional wallop in just a few pages. A gorgeous evocation of loneliness, of the delicate yearning for connection, for contact, at the same time as it pursues larger notions of manhood. Lovely and deeply memorable."

—**Megan Abbott**, Short Fiction Judge, Fall 2015

FIRST RULE, HE makes sure to look in the lady's eyes when he smiles. Second, he crinkles his like Clint Eastwood. Tonight, many nights, he practices his smile in the tri-fold mirror, locks the bathroom door so his four-year-old can't get in. He thinks of that Eastwood who could swagger about with a rifle in hand, but could also touch a lady, tender, at the small of her back. Who could work rugged days, eyes creased by the sun, but also meet you with a word, warm and measured. Eastwood once said, *manhood is really a quiet thing*.

•••

He meets a lady now and then. A new clerk at the burger joint, the one close enough for morning break. Or at the liquor mart, there always seems to be a different set of hands stocking his rolling paper. Then there's the drug tech. Transferred from the next county, now she's the one who measures out his wife's monthly dose of meds. Last month, when the tech turned away to retrieve the pills, he could see a scar on her cheek, a tiny furrow where a scratch once healed.

When he talks to a lady, he touches the table or the counter where she stands—as if the surface were made of hardwood oak and his fingertip traces the grains. He favors the ring finger. Of the five digits, the ring finger has the gentlest touch. *Reed-like and gentle.* He heard Della say that once. His wife. In her brief Mary Kay venture, advising homemakers on how to dab and daub, all with the softest of touches.

•••

From the living room comes the sound of a sitcom laugh track, the repeated rumbling like a hungry belly. He knows the scene well. His wife and two daughters lounge on the floor, their faces close to the TV screen, heads propped up by their hands. Della refuses to open the curtains, and she has stripped all of the bulbs from the living room lamps; he can't find where she's put them. And now, all the cigarette smoke that she's exhaled through the day— it collects, catching in the brightness of the television. A foggy-blue palette shades the room, and there, his daughters and Della lie, their heads of dark hair dimpled with plastic curlers.

Later, when they've turned in for the night, he looks in on them sleeping—Della, the two girls—all three piled together in the twin bed. They still wear the rollers in their hair. Plastic the color of cornflowers.

As for himself, he will settle into the living room couch. The infomercials have begun, *with a deal you just won't believe.* He presses the mute button and lets his eyes grow heavy. Even as he drifts, he can see the light of the TV flashing quickly. It flickers along his eyelids, like sunlight through a canopy of leaves.

•••

The next day, the pharmacy is awash with fluorescence. He allows several people to go ahead of him in line, trying to wangle a quiet meeting with the drug tech. When he reaches the counter, he smiles; he looks in her eyes, and she lets him. It's been a month—exactly thirty days—but, he thinks, couldn't she remember him?

"What was the name?" she asks.

It's the standard greeting, the line she's used for every customer so far. But maybe, given the chance, she'll remember his eyes.

"I'm here for Della," he tells her. *Smile again, crinkle the eyes.* "Della Lee."

The tech nods and turns away, disappearing into the rows of ordered pills.

In front of him, the counter is pure white, but he commences his tracing as if it were oak. Those furrows of the wood grains, he can almost feel them. *How many rings wound around its trunk?* His fingertip traces, traces. His knuckle flexes. And, glinting with each move, his gold wedding band.

"Sir?" The tech is looking at him expectantly.

She passes him a white paper sack, the pills inside shifting and rattling, and as he pays, his hand grazes her skin. Accidental, imprecise, his touch lands—*was that her finger, her palm?* A small and soft collision. But he can feel the kickback. It travels up his arm, into his chest.

•••

As a boy, he used to trek with his father along the woods' edge, where the ashes and oak grow heavy. Their rifles were close at hand. The ammo inside its pack shifted and rattled.

In the long, quiet stretches when there were no bucks, sometimes a doe would whisper past, her coat flickering with the sunlight as it slanted through the canopy. He and his father just watched, and her muscles would tighten then soften, tighten then soften as she moved.

His father taught: some lines are sacred. The does were on one side, the men on the other. *Most seasons*, his father would say, *you can't hold fast to a doe. She raises the young. She's protected. All you can do is to tip your hat to her.* And his father would touch the brim of his cap. *Let her slow-dance right past.*

He and his father, they always brought home more mottos and ammo than meat.

•••

That night. Della's white paper sack delivered. The bathroom door locked. He goes through the motions. *Smile again, crinkle the eyes.*

Pink Mary Kay bottles, unsold, line up along bathtub ledge, and he pours a drop of lotion on his left wrist, smoothing the pale cream up his hand. When he reaches his fingers, he takes care around his ring, pays close attention to the fleshy lines at his knuckles. He works the cream into his skin until all that remains is a slight oily sheen. Then he does the right hand.

His wife dabs lotion daily. He's watched her. She stands in this spot, where he does now, and gazes into the tri-fold mirror. Dabbing at the cream, dabbing at her skin. She uses only her ring finger.

•••

Behind the mirror, tucked away, sits a small notebook. Inside, the scribbles of her cosmetic training. He used to open the pages, hoping to find some clue to Della's state of mind. The pages stayed bare, except for the first few, where the paper is rumpled from moisture and wear.

Ring finger, she wrote in her slanted script. *The ring finger—long & delicate like a reed. It is the weakest and has the gentlest touch. Try using it. You might have to try over & over. Might be hard to manage at first. Weakness allows it to be gentle. Gentle & wild—both.*

•••

In the living room, he sits on the couch, rolls several cigarettes before lighting one for himself. All through the evening, tobacco smoke trails from Della's mouth; ash falls from her fingertips. He and Della and their girls eat dinner by blue-gray light.

At midnight, the plates still lie on the rug, caked in grease, and in the silver fog, the wife and girls start gathering for *goodnights*. There are no kisses, just the three of them filing past him. They murmur and sigh, and he lifts his hand in a sort of a wave. As with every bedtime, he watches them make their way down the hall, hair all rolled up in those matching curlers. And tonight, he smiles to himself. Just smiles. Because it looks to him that Della, his girls—atop each of their heads sits a crown made of petals. Cornflower blue. Yes, for a moment, against the darkness of the hallway, he can see those blue flowers and can see them flicker, then glow.

THE IMMACULATE HEART OF MARY STEEL CITY, 1910

INGRID JENDRZEJEWSKI

"'The Immaculate Heart of Mary / Steel City 1910' honors the form of flash fiction by not attempting to make it something it isn't: it's neither a boiled down short story nor a fleeting glimpse of life. She manages to evoke the grittiness and toil of early twentieth century immigrant life and the complexities of gender and desire in a piece filled with magic, lust, and despair. This story won my (far from immaculate) heart."

—**Anne Finger**, Flash Fiction Judge, Fall 2015

MAGDA DESCENDS ON Polish Hill like so much of the metal whose siren song lured our fathers and grandfathers away from their *matki* and motherland. Within a week, she is selling newspapers on the street corners. Within two, she has us organized.

We wear our brothers' clothing, we cut our hair. She teaches us to spit; we forget our breasts. She brings us papers and we sell them. We take our pennies, she takes a cut.

At first, we are ecstatic: we can now turn paper into copper into bread. Our fathers may wring coins from steel but their kind of money is passed to the old country, evaporating like our memories of the words of the *Bogurodzica*.

But then things start to shift. One by one, we feel a dent, notice a hollow. We begin to feel a missing. When we walk, our chests crackle.

And sure enough, when we look, we find that our hearts are gone. Our chests are filled with crumpled newsprint. We float when we walk because there is nothing to weigh us down, but it is a lightness that makes us feel heavy.

Magda lives near the *Kościół Matki Boskiej* and when I pass it, I hear the blood beat through its domes. I make the sign of the cross. She is not at home when I arrive, but there is no lock on the door and I let myself in.

Her room is small so I see them immediately: our hearts are wrapped in newspaper, lined up in rows along the floorboards. I look for mine, but it is not with the others. I find it elsewhere, near her pillow, in her bed. It looks as if it has been used.

I want to seize it, free it, take back what is mine. But when my hand brushes Magda's sheets, I find myself unable to move. There are nickels in my pockets and I am thinking about love.

I will stand here until Magda returns, until I am sure of my own mind. I will stand here while the bells of the Immaculate Heart of Mary ring in the eventide, until the blood in my veins is black and thick like ink.

FLIGHT THEORY

ALLISON ADAIR

"The poem pulled me into [the speaker's] experience from the first two lines. The writer grapples with the complexity of her experience by using language that is rough, raw, surprising, painful and difficult, but important. The poem is layered and full of imaginings, it places the reader right there in the moment. The writer builds the images and follows them to one surprising, frightful, gorgeous conclusion."

—**Cheryl Boyce-Taylor**, Poetry Judge, Fall 2015

Gorlice 1908

Wstawaj, don't You turn off the lights this time and
speak, he will lie still, a body shifting from its country,
wake, and come climb gaunt gray waves into a sky built
for you. My hand deep within the fat matter of memory. Stirring
over your mouth is his tongue, he slips into your wet speech,
our goodbye. dismantles you quietly, rot threading plaster.

His black Organs are everywhere: on the workbench outside
feathers stir, no animals left unskinned. Empty socket stuffed with
wind, oil upon a dirty rag, only you know about the snake
oil, his long beak pushing through high grass. He'll slough until the world
shines. Take this, offers an indifferent body. (Who can be choosy?)
I have saved This, your life—what is a stepfather for? For emptying

it all slowly in a ribcage, the warm meat of your parts lost as
a shoe, zrób co his hands undo—your mother will say wings, whispering, but
mówię, lodge it in truth—you lose yourself under a loud human neck,
in the gathers its gulping skin stretched over bones, over low vowels
at your waist and you pray no one hears, not even you. These voices, glottal,
never exhale. they travel with you, to Kraków, Hamburg, Cuxhaven, Nowy Jork,

Run, road to station to the factory where you cart bobbins in a skirt, again and again
to the dim nodding ship. arriving full, departing empty: sound rimming the lip of a bell.
Szybko. You will know no Windows too narrow to let the light in. Dark swells
one. If you hear me in your quiet inner room, like a mushroom sponging into root.
calling you, moja New world daughter threaded with horsehair worms, their
córka, close the small farm sprouting even under your fingernail. Once you had a

door to us. Run past: the tremoring kerosene lamps, the hard stone roads still
until dark birds come for you. But now shadows buckle into static, a man sent to
hang, shoreless, the distant tin-foil moon, doing nothing but walking, without gravity.
aimless, land As if ours were a small world, well lit, the sounds you hear only footsteps
disappearing like salt across the dust of a slackening galaxy; you, a mass of ice slow-spiraling.
in a stirred glass. Your young son flaps from the screen, *what is it like, Mamusia, to float
away?*

GONER

BETH ANN FENNELLY

"The author uses ecclesiastical language to great effect, as it immediately establishes that this setting is a world apart. Yet, at the same time, given this author's compelling language—the vivid, potent, and compelling details—the narrator invites the reader inside this narrative. I should also hasten to add that the author is a beautiful stylist. She seamlessly twines together themes of sexual abuse and gender politics. Within these themes, she also uses irony to great effect. This is a winning essay!"

—**Sue William Silverman**, Creative Nonfiction Judge, Fall 2015

THAT FRIDAY, AFTER morning mass, the priests visited our third grade to announce a meeting for prospective altar boys.

I went. Me, a girl. Why did I go? First, I was attracted to the theatrics: the costuming with the alb and the cincture, the stately procession down the aisle with the cross and the thurible (the censer filled with incense) that one of the altar boys (the thurifer) swung on its Jacob Marley chains. I wanted to arrange the credence table—the corporal, the cruet, and the ciborium. I wanted to hold the ewer of holy water into which the priest dipped the aspergillum and then flicked it, raining holiness on penitent heads. When the priest held the Eucharist up, I wanted to twist the cluster of brass sanctus bells, alerting the congregation to the mystery of transubstantiation, that moment when the bread and wine were miracled into Body and Blood. And clearly I wanted to fill the chalice of my mouth with the wine of those words. Thurible and aspergillum and ciborium. The purificator, the paten and the pall.

Also, I went to prove a point: I shouldn't be excluded because I was a girl.

But I never got the chance. Before the meeting began, Father Mayer evicted me from the front pew. "I'll be right back," he told my classmates, then steered me by my shoulder to the sacristy where, behind a heavy door, a few bent old ladies were ironing. *This is the altar society*, he told me. *These women care for the priestly vestments. This is where God calls you to serve.* He fled, and I fled, and that evening I wrote a letter in my best penmanship tattling on him to Cardinal Joseph Bernadin—girls should be altar servers! Women should be priests!

My mom loved the letter and saved it, how cute, the little women's libber. It didn't occur to me at the time that her saving the letter meant she'd never sent it.

Now, a grown woman with children of my own, back in Illinois at my mother's table, I read in *The Trib* that church files released in 2014 show that Father Mayer sexually abused altar boys for decades. At each parish, accusations, followed by a new assignment. He'd been removed from St. Mary's and sent to St. Edna's, removed from St. Edna's and sent to St. Stephen's, removed from St. Stephen's and sent to St. Dionysius's, removed from St. Dionysius' and sent to St. Odilo's. All those altered boys. Did the archdiocese, the Cardinal, know? *Please.* In the files, there's a contract Bernadin made Fr. Mayer sign, promising that at St. Odilo's he wouldn't be alone with boys younger than twenty-one. Because by then two of his altar boys had committed suicide.

After St. Odilo's, he was sent to jail.

You can look all of this up, if you care to. Father Robert E. Mayer, pastor of St. Mary's, Lake Forest, Illinois, from 1975 to 1981. Call this fiction: I dare you.

I lay the newspaper down in a light that is no longer the light of my mother's kitchen, but is the stained light of St. Mary's, where solid pillars of dust used to prop up the clerestory windows, and in this light I see it all anew, I see it all anew, and clear as a bell, as we say, as if cued by altar boys twisting the sanctus bells, announcing that something has been transubstantiated into something else, forever. The meeting where Fr. Mayer shoved me into the sacristy where the ironing women lifted the blank communion wafers of their faces. The click of dress shoes as he rushed back to the meeting, his robes streaming behind him like wings. Followed by, a few years later, his sudden "sabbatical." His goodbye potluck.

My outrage at not being chosen. My bad luck at being born a girl.

My classmate Donny O'Dell, who *was* chosen, during mass that unseasonably warm Easter—he was holding high the Bible, rigid and dutiful, when suddenly he toppled backward. The whole congregation heard the sickening thwack of skull on marble, and as one, we uttered the same surprised *Oh!*—as if it were part of the mass, as if a response had been inserted before the Agnus Dei—*Oh!* we cried, in a single voice—and how quickly good Father Mayer was at his side, bending, lifting in his arms the small boy, Donny O'Dell, a boy even smaller than I was, Donny in his arms like Jesus removed from his cross, or, with his white alb flowing toward the floor, like a bride. And how Donny raised a hand to his head and opened his eyes and realized that he'd fainted and smiled a sheepish smile. How the parishioners laughed a relieved laugh to see he was okay. How later, filing out into the narthex, everyone laughed again with Mrs. O'Dell. *Your son gave us quite a scare, Nance. For a moment, we thought he was a goner.*

FICTION

EDITED BY SEAN BERNARD

FICTION

SPELL FOR MAKING A WEREWOLF

LISA LOCASCIO

THE NAKED GIRL takes you into a small bathroom with a crowded yellowy marble vanity. Vials of hair oil, all-natural toothpaste, a bottle of cider vinegar, a stubby gray eyeliner from her old lover's mother.

She makes a perfunctory show of tidying. Holds a wad of toilet paper under a blast of water from the swanning tap, wipes against the marble's white streaks. Drops makeup into various pouches, asserts a hegemony of washes and creams. Then, with a bored look, she opens a small drawer—the bottom one, which is poorly installed and does not draw well—and withdraws a corded tool of light shiny plastic. The naked girl sets it up on the counter: a baby pink Lady Hygiene trimmer. You had the exact same one, until the blade rusted and you went back to waxing.

She plugs the trimmer in. Moves her finger over the switch. When the buzzing starts you realize how quiet you've been, even holding your breath. Now the air is unbearably loud. You flush, but it feels more like a flash. You're drenched. You fan.

The naked girl pivots her pelvis to the sink and begins to shave her pubic hair in neat steady rows. Down and up, left to right. She watches intently in the mirror, sometimes thrusting to adjust the angle of her jut. Scattered hair falls in the sink, which is rimmed with streams of brown slime and traces of some manner of sand.

"I can come to you," the naked girl says without looking up. "Come into you. Enter you. Any time I want."

You want to ask her what she means, but the Lady Hygiene trimmer is nearing her labia majora, and you realize you've been holding your breath again.

"If you hold someone in your mind they will stay with you," she says. "As long as you want."

Be careful, you want to yelp, but you are silent as she closes her eyes and moves the Lady Hygiene between her legs, spreading her lips with the fingers of her left hand, and presses it straight up against her body. Stare incredulously at her rosy, purple-veined eyelids. For a minute—for many—you're certain she's going to take the trimmer inside her body. That it will disappear into her and blood will seep ineluctably and you'll have to call an ambulance.

Where is your phone, anyway? You look for the door but can't see it. You feel a headache coming on. Look and look for the door, turning in a small circle. The naked girl shaves blindly on. When your circle is complete, she has climbed up on the sink, spread eagle over the basin, as if inviting the faucet to penetrate her. Now her eyes are open, trained intently on the supple bloom of her minora, around which the Lady Hygiene traces a careful perimeter.

"If you hold someone in your mind you can have them, is all I'm trying to say," she tells you. "Have anything you want with them."

You want to ask what she wants but you can't speak.

She smirks, looking at you for the first time. "Hand me that mug," she says.

Suddenly the room is bigger. The Lady Hygiene trimmer has stopped buzzing. Without thinking you check and see she is done shaving. Then, horrified, you mumble an apology, which the naked girl ignores.

The mug is on the vanity, not ceramic but a thick dull plastic in a shade of orange with which you have a difficult history. An orange from your animal time, from the meshes of earliest childhood. A shade of magic marker that made you want to vomit. You never saw it anywhere else, and you wondered if that was what made the markers magic—that orange's nausea. All the other colors washed from the side of your left hand, the one you dragged through every drawing, but the orange was stubborn as a curse. And then one day it blessedly disappeared. A different kind of magic. They don't even seem to make that color anymore. You hand the naked girl the mug, repressing the desire to vomit. If you do, at least you're in a bathroom, you think.

She peers into the mug and holds it out so that you will peer into it, too. The bottom is covered in scattered patches of brown scum floating in yellowy water. The naked girl swipes her finger through the sink, scraping what it catches into the mug. Maybe an ounce of her golden hair, some of the sand stuff, and the sink slime, a different brown than the scum.

"I keep my toothbrush in here," the girl says, and takes a small carton of milk from the bottles assembled on the vanity. It's the very same kind of milk carton that they served in your grade school cafeteria. How did you miss it before? Everyone whose parents had paid for milk was entitled to two little cartons from the oversize fridge in the room next to the gym. Also in the fridge were allergy medicines for children so afflicted, and hardened PB&Js for kids who forgot their lunches. By fourth grade you knew that you could take two milks even though your parents hadn't paid, even though the reason they hadn't was because you had told them that you didn't like milk. You could go in that fridge and take as many milks as you wanted. Nobody kept track.

You haven't seen a carton like that since. And now, here it is, on the naked girl's sink.

Who is she again? How did you get here? When you try to remember, the curtains in your head slam shut.

The naked girl pushes the carton's snout open—the seal was already broken, it has been sitting on the counter like that, unrefrigerated, which can't be healthy—and pours a few ounces of milk into the mug. Swishes it with one hand, splashing hair-milk over the edges. Then she lowers it between her legs and you think she's going to pee into it but instead she just scrapes in more hair shavings, giving you a feeling of perverse relief.

Then she pees into it. Not a lot—you're amazed by her control—only a shot glass worth of urine, you estimate.

Some part of your consciousness is sparking, stuck. The naked girl is tilting her vomit-orange mug of hair-milk to your mouth.

"Bottoms up," she says.

When you open your lips she tips it all in. The best thing you can think to say is that it doesn't taste as bad as you imagined. But when you search your thoughts for what you imagined, there's nothing there.

"Swallow," the naked girl says. "I want you to shave my neck."

Something claps and you find yourself on tiptoes behind her, trimming her nape with Lady Hygiene. There's nothing in your mouth anymore.

"Farther," she says, pressing back into you. "Further."

When you've shaved up to the widest point of her skull, you think it prudent to stop, and do so without asking or even turning the Lady Hygiene off the right way. Just yank the pink plug right out of the wall.

"Have you ever wanted to disappear? I can make you disappear," the girl says without turning. "Lick my head."

When you open your mouth she backs her head into it. Lazily, as if it is not part of you, your tongue drags against her unevenly shaved scalp. Swallow more hair.

"Good boy," she purrs.

I'm not a boy, you want to protest, but she turns around, takes your shoulders in her hands, and sits you down on the open toilet.

"Aren't you, though?" She gazes between your legs. You remember that you, too, are naked. "Aren't you?"

The naked girl pivots back to the mirror over the sink, admiring her newly shorn parts. You don't want to open your mouth for fear she will put something else in it.

"You know why I shave part of my head? Why you shave it?"

Something is not right with your vision. There's a tear between the camera images of your two eyes. Her face jagged and unseeable. You shake your head.

"To show you there's no way out. There's no way around it."

There are tracers in your vision now, flashing incandescent. Your tongue and nose pulse off-and-on numb.

What are you talking about? you want to whisper, your head in your hands. How did it get there?

"There's no way around it," the naked girl repeats, smiling sadly at you. "Me. You."

You're crying now. You can barely see at all.

The naked girl crouches and comes close. Holds a cool hand over your face.

"Close your eyes," she murmurs, and you do. You're so grateful that you want to kiss her. But you haven't the energy.

"None of this is real," she tells you. "Look, the mirror's gone now. The toilet. The sink. The vanity. Even the milk carton. All that's left is you and me."

You breathe, not looking because there is nothing to see.

"That's all." She exhales. "That's all there is. You understand now. Are you tired?"

You're crying so hard you can't breathe.

"Close your eyes," she coos again. "When you wake up, tell me your dreams."

THREE SHORTS

MICHAEL CHANEY

LITTLE FAMILY IN MY SNOWBANK

I HATED TAKING out the skin-stinging trash, an adventure in snow and civics. The path in front of my house led to the driveway the plow guy shaved too close too much. Him, the wolf at my door. The plow man my wife was paranoid of. Him, who kept plowing because every time's another thirty bucks. She pointed out how he'd come even when it hadn't snowed. I know, I know. First world problems. Thing is, she was right. Not only did he knock on the door to collect thirty bucks when it snowed, but he also started to make it snow. Why so much? Why such a big plow blade? And why bee sting yellow? For answers, observe the snow in piles. Mountains of it. A class tax of snow. A-lean-on-my-house of snow. It was as if the plow guy put my lawn under one of those self-serve ice cream machines. He circles the landscaping Styrofoam slow, snowing up the sides, leaving the middle for last. I imagine the plow guy trying to whip the top of his hypothetical sundae (my lawn, mind you). But it's hollow underneath. And if you can imagine all that, then you have an inkling of what I saw as I looked at the snowbank ten feet high—the top of which was sinking ever so perfectly in place, falling into itself. I heard a broken yell. Many plunged trumpets were ready to play within the snowbank. From the top, smoke curled up to the stars. I dropped my trash bag then. There, within Snow Mountain—put on my driveway by my plow man to freak out my wife—was a little family. They had a little fire going in a wee fireplace. It was gooseberry cheerful with matchstick rocking chairs and bottle cap Dutch ovens. A little one was reading a miniature book on the rug. Another was on its back fast asleep. You could hear faint snoring over the ice screaming in your ears. There was a sense, too, of others. Sight unseen. Ready to defend the home fires. I backed away. Anybody would have. This wasn't about fighting. This was about that goddamn plow guy. No wonder he came all the time. Built himself a little igloo condominium for little families to live in, did he? Test my patience (and politics), would he? My wife and I would tell the plow guy not to come any more, wouldn't we? Yes, we'd insist that he take down Snow Mountain, never letting on about how lucrative the rents are here. He didn't come back around for a while. Probably at that "second" job he'd lingered to tell us about that one time. Many days passed with trash to take out, the hideous path to shovel, fatal icicles in the eaves to menace with a broom (closing your eyes each time you make contact, flecked by cold razor dust). One night, I was holding the ladder for my wife. She'd gone up on our roof with her new telescope aimed at the plow guy's house. In between her shouting down at me to keep the ladder steady, I heard a little sound. TV noises coming from the snowbank. Funny thing, what with all that yelling and the TV, I spilled my canteen. Champagne froze the ladder in place so I didn't have to hold on anymore. My wife was still on the roof, looking through her telescope as I tracked the noise, stepping careful to cover the crunch of my boots. I sanctioned the whole thing in my head as I crept. This is my property. I'm a human being and just look at them. They're squatting in a snowbank beside my house on my driveway and it's all been engineered by a plow guy who's making a killing. I thought I would get the shovel and end it, the snowbank with them inside. Everything was blue, the color of darkness whispering your ear off with the cold. The same kind of blue, as it turned out, was coming from that tiny TV set when I looked in on them. Silver shadowed the room as those little ones danced their legs in its shine. They were lying on their bellies on the dog hair rug watching the TV. Snow sparkled where it peeked through their birch bark paneling. The hair on their heads caught the light filament-thin like silk worms suspending from summer trees. So they had a nice living room. So what. I had a shovel. But something in me wanted a flurry of boots instead—a big bad wolf kicking to blow down this precious Norman Rockwell bullshit in my driveway, all brilliantly finagled by the fucking plow guy. Enough! I would end it. But then PGL. Plow Guy Lights. I shouted to my wife using our code. PGL! She didn't answer. Her telescope was trained on me. I could tell by her silhouette against the moon. PGL went the way predicted for our sun—bursting into a giant cymbal crash of whiteness. When you walk through the portal, you wonder momentarily about sand until there is nothing but yellow and all that tidal waving snow.

STEALING HOME DEPOT

I DIDN'T STEAL the whole thing. Only one track of it, a stealer engine maybe. Me, Dogwalker Bill, that's what they called me. Then they called me with a phone. They said I couldn't walk dogs for them anymore and I promised not to lose any more. I promised not to like the sound of chains unlatching. Then they said that was why they were calling. Said they were trying to run a business. I had already let too many go. It was then I was fired. Anyways, I needed a job and was trying to work there at the Home Depot. Actually, I wanted to be a roofer 'cause it sounded good and I like heights, so I went to the Home Depot to get tools in my best sport coat, hoping to make a "good impression." There were mini orange forklifts beeping and just as many people in orange vests as not, pounding on paint cans with rubber mallets or sawing smelly vinyl roller shades or walking slow behind you with their orange aprons on like they were tied to you by some invisible leash. I found the loneliest aisle I could and climbed an orange ladder to get to where they keep hex bolts for going around corners. Then it dawned on me. Why not work here? And so I went to the back looking for an office maybe, and the manager. He'd hand me a piece of paper and see if I got my own pen and when I didn't, I'd borrow his orange one, real polite. And when I couldn't fill it out right there, he'd show me to some stool or chair where I could fill it out and give it back and then jump off a building. All of us together. Manager, pen, me, filled-out paper, and fast receding clouds. We'd form a pattern like skydivers in the shape of a crankshaft. I was going to go back there to do all that. Whenever you go where you're not supposed to be it looks very interesting no matter what. There's a bathroom in the back of the grocery store that I go to. To get there you have to pass through a gate made of long strips of heavy dirty plastic, the kind the back wheels of semi trucks have to keep the rain off the tires. You feel like unwanted rain when you go in there. At the back of the Home Depot was only a door, not orange, and no flaps. The room it opened to was big, empty. I felt like a mouse who'd just crawled into some old lady's ranch house garage, the rakes and shovels labeled and dangling from yarn knots on church white pegboard. I scampered along the sawdust until I passed what I thought was the bathroom and another door. I knocked and somebody shouted "Command!" So I shouted "Get a job!" I was going to keep on, but the door opened. It was the manager with some nervous guy in a chair, almost a kid, and another guy: older, fatter than the manager, dressed like a cop. The cop laughed and patted my arm like we were friends saying, "Well, here he is." He showed me the kid like he was mine. Before any talk of payments, I was going to say the kid looked nothing like me. Plus, I was only here for the job. But I didn't have to on account of them nodding so much. To them, I was on the job already. I tugged on the collars of my sport coat to make sure I was still making a good impression. I must have been because they told me real slow and real serious how the kid, head in hands, had taken something from the Home Depot. It left them no choice but to call me. The kid wouldn't sign all the orange forms they wanted him to. They said more about security cameras and how glad they were I was there. I only nodded. The manager agreed and said that my partner was going to come for the paperwork afterwards like it was a question. I only nodded. He nodded more too. That must have been the cure, because once the cop shoved the kid up, out of the chair, and toward me—just like that, the pain in my chest was gone. When I turned around and walked back to the memory of the plastic strips, the kid was trailing me like a dropped leash. It was then he shot me a look. He was sorry or guilty or maybe something else. I saw him go, tail between his legs, checking out through the express lane. I was feeling victorious. Another job well done and all that. I thought I'd take my time. Self checkout. I got two hex bolts on the glass and two in my pocket, snug in there with their magnetic little shock collars set and ready to spring at the automatic doors. They sigh so impatiently just before it happens.

AND NOT A DROP TO DRINK

I KEEP HAVING this terroir where I wake up endoftheworld slaked of thirst. Buckets of water wouldn't quench the mouthful of sand I got. I'd probably drown first. So I scramble out of bed and as soon as I open the door, instead of the stairs, it's E. 59th St.—the late night gas station on the corner unafraid. I go there for liquid large as buckets. I'm blue tongue thirsty. Bad day in hell thirsty. I step into the station and out of the humming streetlights that want to show me cigarette stubs linting an old blanket of concrete at the threshold. For a few open door seconds, necrotic fluorescents sing along to mosquito music. None of it does anything for my thirst. I walk in and a key lime sign comes for me. A hot dog perfectly murdered with mustard. There are no words for the optic tang. There's also the plastic shimmer of the scratch ticket rotisseries by the counter. There *are* words for those. "Scam" is one. "Empty" is another, because they are. So is the counter. No one's here. The security camera monitor is in the corner. Instead of showing me in grainy dot matrix walking by dusted motor oils and freshly squeezed bread, a cartoon plays. A cat goes for a bird but grabs hot sauce by accident, drinking it to burstingredfaced proportions, and then runs to chug a bottle of not-water given that huge skull on the label, Hans Holbein huge. But I don't care. I'm only interested in the back corner. They keep liquids there: smoky cold behind glass—but not the new cases that open smoother than Enterprise bay doors and close slow on their own like hermit crabs. No, these have heavy louver doors. They won't slide against the muck in the tracks, that catch and bump build-up in the tracks going back to glass bottle days of tin pulltabs and penny candy. Sliding one of these glass anvils over to get the armfuls of liquid I need is going to be a bicep challenge. I think I may have to stretch out first. Maybe do some jogging in place before I rip these coolers open and get those drinks. Why *not* do some light calisthenics? The attendant still isn't there by the razed forest of lotto dispensaries stumping the counter. But then I notice the drinks through the battleship's portal plexiglass of the cooler. Where I think I'll see the usual waters, plus or minus sugar and bubble, there's nothing but cheese-flavored beverages. A colonnade of them, shiny and absurd in their rows. There's 'VARTI, the Martian martini, and bottles upon bottles of Garden of Edam. Pre-lactasean: their culture's double cream, cheese curd, no mite, Dutch-type, no ammoniated cow waters they. Only cave aged, barrel block, blue vein. Lock tight. Nacho crock. Coco-Colby. More affinage than bloomy. Chevre Chalk and RIND! "That Muenster Flavor Without the Monster Aftertaste." Gouda-ade. Swiss—BLIND! And Big Barny. Grated microbial. Lipase. CHEDDA! Got curdling? Yeah, well these got it too. So do the pictures on their labels. It's a cutesy caseophilia for the eyes. A real turophile freak show full of smiling wedges and orange winklings, extra sharp. One can of Dr. Jack has a whole story printed on it about

Benjamin Franklin "distilling the fine ichor, the very essence of cheese." On the front is a googly-eyed red pepper in a sombrero and bandoleers firing off cans of the stuff (the font for the BANG of the first gun is made up of little buttery wedges, flecked green and red). Garden of Edam: Large Curd shows Eve in a medieval triptych, learning from the snake how to milk, brick, and then remilk cheese—"so refreshing, it's sinful." But I don't want to read anymore, or watch cartoons, or be dreaming anything so gross. All I want is something to drink. The dryness of my mouth is the hole in the ozone. It wants the stock market to crash. It hates freedom and all will be exposed in Thirsty-Gate and the media attention will solve the world's famine, I'm sure, but in the meantime, *who is going to get me something to fucking drink?* Then I notice a stray picture on a label of Briesca. A bunch of cans all in a row, a special shape, so special that upon seeing it I instantly know what I have to do. I begin robbing the cases of their worthless bottles and cans, their jugs and cartons. I open all the lids and pull off all the tabs and turn and twist all the caps. The vessels hiss at me, hiccuping and shushing, in proof of the classic tomes "that the possessed speak in a language unbeknownst to him or her." Behold, the power of cheese (compels you). But I know that's not it. That shit doesn't exist except in commercials and church and I'm certain of it now more than ever. Before I light the fuses, the containers whistle more blasphemies up to the popcorn ceiling tiles. I'm still thirsty, but at least the cheese is free.

TUNNEL

GLEN POURCIAU

I'M IN MY own house minding my own business when someone knocks on the front door. I hate it when someone knocks because well over half the time it's a nuisance knock, but I make a trip to the peephole to be sure. It's a next-door neighbor we've never met, the man of the family that in the six months since it moved in has caused a nagging sense of encroachment on our peace of mind.

Every weekend this family receives legions of visitors, presumably relatives, who arrive in almost identical SUVs that remain parked in a long line in front of our houses for one night, sometimes two. They pour out of the SUVs brandishing smartphones, and a prolonged series of ritual hugging follows, most of the huggers checking their phones over the other person's shoulder. On the way up the walk they seem giddy as they poke their phones and talk at the same time. They gather in the backyard around the pool and play music or sports over their sound system, their noise sucking up all the air around our thoughts whenever we walk out the back door. I haven't taken a look over the eight-foot fence separating our yards, but one recent day I did see my knocking neighbor's pregnant wife and their two four-foot-tall children and the tiny one in the stroller waiting at the bus stop, fascinating themselves with their devices. Even the kid in the stroller was vigorously slapping a rectangular screen.

But in the interest of fairness and respect, I open the door just as the neighbor raises his fist to knock again. He identifies himself as my neighbor, tells me his name, and apologizes for taking so long to introduce himself. He pauses, so I tell him my name and shake his hand, wondering what he might expect of me. Does he think I should invite him in? I feel no inclination to do so, and I don't call for Denise to come to the door to meet him.

In fact I dread that she'll hear us, walk up from behind and ask him to come in for a chat, so I step out onto the porch and shut the door. I've already forgotten his name, but it's more accurate to say I never remembered it in the first place. I don't like the look of him, too self-consciously friendly, a self-serving paternalism that is meant to put me at ease but has the opposite effect, an air of superiority and entitlement he embodies with such purity that I think he must have been born with it. I suspect he may be here to sell me something. He cares nothing about the answers to the questions he asks—where I'm from, how long we've lived in the neighborhood, what I do or used to do for a living, do we have children? For my part I don't care to answer his questions, though I do reply briefly, no kids, retired public servant and so forth, but I don't prolong his visit by asking similar questions about him and his family.

"I hope you're not bothered by all the parking we have going on out here on the weekends. We're big believers in family, and we want to share our good fortune with them. We feel like we're living the dream and we want our loved ones right here in the dream with us."

He expects these comments to charm me, but the dawning spell is broken when his phone vibrates in his pocket. He excuses himself, lifts the phone out, peeks, pokes something on the phone and puts it away.

"You won't hear that again," he assures me. "I wouldn't want us to be interrupted when I ask you this." He looks me in the eye, hoping I'll smile at him, but I don't. "This is a little awkward, but believe me, I have generous intentions. Our family loves it here, and both sides, mine and my wife's, parents and brothers and sisters, like to come over so all of us can be together. We cook for one another, and all the kids are there, you must have seen them, generations all under the same roof, all a great pleasure to us, as you can imagine." He pauses again, eyeing me. "The problem is that we're a little crowded, and I'd guess that the number of people we have in our house could at times create some discomfort for you and your wife. I apologize for that, but I've thought of a possible solution. The timing may not be right for you, but I don't know unless I ask, do I? So this is my proposal or question, I'm not sure which word fits best. Have you and your wife ever thought of downsizing? It could be that you've considered it already, but I see the look on your face and I take it that this idea strikes you as out of the blue. I don't mean to be rude, but hear me out for a moment. We'd be willing to make you a more than reasonable offer for your home. We can work together on this, find out what houses are selling for in the area, and we'd add a bonus. That would only be fair since you have a great bargaining advantage here. You own the exact piece of property we want, you don't have a for-sale sign in the yard and you've shown no previous inclination to sell. You may be asking yourself why it has to be this property. Because we like it here and we'd rather not move again. We don't have the resources to buy some grandiose home, but we need more room to accommodate the family. Unfortunately the house on our west side has two levels, and we prefer a one-story house because it's better for our parents. They've got knee and hip replacements to think about, plus the kids running up and down the stairs while checking their phones seems risky to us, they could step off into mid-air. Our plan is to construct an adjoining hallway between the two houses, one that we could all use to go back and forth in all kinds of weather, and we'd take the fence down between the yards to create sort of a mini-campus for us to roam around in, the pool being complemented by what would be the garden in what is now your backyard. Of course you can understand how excited we are thinking of the possibilities, but I told Lucille we shouldn't get too far ahead of ourselves, I should go next door and see if any of this has a chance of becoming real. So tell me, are you at least open to discussing this with your wife? I know it will take time, and we'd have to talk more. You'd need to find another place to live, obviously, and I know excellent people who can help you with that."

Finished, he takes a good look at me, and in his own face I see resentment. It's resentment that I'm not reacting to his proposal more openly and graciously, as if putting my desires above his implies a stubborn self-centeredness. The idea that he'll hold a refusal against us makes me want to throw him off our little front porch, but instead I go back in the house and straight to Denise to tell her the story.

"Are you sure that's what he said?" She's on the screened porch reading, music from the other side of the fence intruding into our conversation.

"I know what I heard, and he didn't like it when I didn't reply. Where do they get the presumptuous gall? This must be connected in some way to their proclivity for reproduction."

"You're losing me now."

"He sees us as being past all that and therefore less vital than he is. In his eyes, our standing ranks inherently lower than his. Just think about it."

Denise gazes at me. She occasionally expresses worry that the anesthesia from my double-hernia surgery six months ago has affected my mind. Just then the music coming from next door becomes louder, and our eyes cut toward it.

We haven't heard anything from our neighbor in a week or two, but several fence pickets in the side yard between our houses have been removed and propped up. I show Denise the pickets, which are outside our bedroom, and tell her my suspicions: that I think they've had someone over to estimate the cost of an adjoining hallway. She wants me to lower my voice, but I don't care if they overhear me. She waves me back in the house, and I follow her.

"Why would they do that?" she asks when we're inside. "Are you sure he understood you?"

"Why are you asking me again if I'm sure what happened? They simply don't care what we want. He may knock on the door again and present us with an offer. Whatever plans they have, we're not included in them, except as ex-neighbors."

•••

Our home is where we live our lives. It is our space, our world, not theirs for the taking. We cannot sit still for any encroachment of our boundaries.

This weekend I'm certain that the whole range of generations is over there imagining what our place looks like on the inside—what kind of appliances and countertops we have, whether our bathrooms are dated and if the carpet will need to be ripped out.

Denise is telling me the itinerary of a driving trip she's been planning, which will take us through New Mexico, Arizona, Utah, and across Nevada into California. She's made reservations for us in several national parks. But as she speaks we hear a distracting noise coming from their house. We go to the fence, and Denise agrees with me that the racket seems to be coming from the part of the house closest to us.

"It sounds like jackhammering," I say.

"They could be looking for a water leak somewhere in the slab."

"But there's no plumber's truck out front."

I go out the back gate and take the short walk down the alley. A white van with no lettering is parked in the driveway and the garage door is up. I see no one and don't want to seem nosy or to get into an angry discussion with anyone. I hurry back and tell Denise about the truck.

"Inconclusive then."

"It's not inconclusive that it's a jackhammer."

"I don't see that it needs to concern us."

I disagree, but I say nothing.

"I'll leave you to it then," she says and goes inside.

I stay near the side fence, my mind working. Eventually I go in and ask Denise if she wants to go to the grocery store with me. As I expect, she says she'd rather sit in her chair and read.

I stop on my way and buy three baseball bats. I've never owned firearms, but I do keep a bat under our bed. I don't know how I'll explain the bats to Denise, but I want them in different parts of the house, just in case.

Denise is in the kitchen when I get home and she gives me a questioning look when she sees the bats.

"I might not need them, but I'll be more comfortable having them around the house."

"Do you imagine we're being invaded?"

"Do you think this is imaginary?"

"I'm sure you're imagining something."

"It doesn't make me wrong."

Several days after the jackhammering I hear knocking. Denise is in the bathroom with the water running and I don't know if she hears it. I tiptoe up to the front door to check the peephole and see our neighbor, straining to keep up his smile. I decide not to speak to him, but I stay put at the door. He knocks again, staring into the peephole with determination before he walks off.

"Who was that?" Denise asks from behind me.

"It was him. I didn't open up. I've got nothing to say to him."

"Maybe he wanted to make an offer on the house."

"I'm not interested in any offer."

"It wouldn't hurt to listen to what he has to say."

I don't answer her, but I don't like the question left in the silence. Would she consider an offer from him?

Denise returns to the bathroom. I pace around and then get my utility ladder and carry it out back. I set it up close to the gap in the fence and climb up, steadying myself with a metal post. The ground has been cleared on the other side of the detached part and a chalk outline has been drawn on the brick in the shape of what could become an opening. Our fences connect and run perpendicular to our houses in front, blocking the view of our side yards from the street, but despite that I can't imagine him being reckless enough to begin construction on a hallway. Has he foreseen that I would look over the fence? Is his purpose to make their plan seem more real to me, to harass and intimidate me? Does he want me to envision workmen crashing through the west wall of our bedroom, wearing goggles and hardhats, toting power tools and sledgehammers?

The family gatherings continue. Their noise seems to be getting louder, but Denise says it's just my nerves.

I think toward our trip in the weeks ahead. I worry what we'll find when we return if we leave our house unoccupied.

Monday morning I see the family waiting for the school bus, their faces drawn to their phones. As I watch from the front window the wife, Lucille, looks up at me, scowling, her finger suspended in the air.

Late in the afternoon I hear knocking again, and this time I don't go to the door. I'm at my desk, reading a news site on the computer, but soon I hear our door open and Denise's voice. I shut my eyes and tell myself to be patient, to not let anger show in my voice when

I speak to her. I imagine his family filing through the under-construction adjoining hall-way, rolling luggage in one hand and thumbing messages on smartphones in the other. I see myself waiting with a bat on my shoulder for the first sledgehammer to crash through our bedroom wall.

Denise appears in my doorway holding a slip of paper.

"He's given us the price they'd pay, he and his relatives, and it's more than the house is worth. He says they can give us half the amount in cash."

She comes toward me and tries to show me the number on the paper, but I shake my head.

"He made it a point to smile a lot, but I didn't like his attitude," she says. "I agree with you, he definitely wants us out."

"What did you tell him?"

"Not a thing, and I didn't look at the number while he was standing there. I don't have any idea of moving anywhere else, especially after listening to him."

"They'll no doubt continue to reproduce."

"That will be true wherever they are."

● ● ●

When Denise is in the shower I take the ladder out and scan their backyard, on the lookout for piles of dirt and rock or elevated levels of dirt in their beds. I see a wheelbarrow and a mound of unearthed dirt and chunks of soiled white rocks by the north side of the fence, but I can see no sign of digging anywhere in the yard.

I climb down, take the ladder in and put it away. I pace until the water in the shower goes off. I stop pacing then and go to my study, my thoughts grinding on the dirt, the offer, the propped-up pickets, and our vacant house.

Denise's voice startles me. She's standing in the doorway of my study. I'm at my desk, facing the computer, its screen gone black because it's been awhile since I touched the key-board.

"Are you thinking about him?"

"There's a big pile of dirt in their side yard."

"What are you saying?"

"I'd like to know more about the dirt."

"If they had a leak, it may be dirt the plumber dug up."

"Why would the plumber leave it in their yard?"

Denise sighs. I don't want her sigh to bother me, but it does. I can understand why she'd sigh, and I can't say anything that would make her want to take it back.

"You think they're digging a tunnel, don't you?"

"I don't know."

"Why would they start the tunnel before making us their offer?"

"He knew I didn't want to sell, but he decided to take his best shot before they dug any farther."

"You're over the top on this, Galen."

"Could be, but this is our place, not theirs."

I patrol the side yard, listening, sometimes hearing their music and laughter. I can't stay up around the clock, but each night before we turn out the lights I walk the area and drop to my hands and knees, feeling the ground for vibrations. Nothing.

As the trip gets closer I find it more difficult to sleep. Denise fears we won't be able to enjoy ourselves while we're away. She argues, her agitation showing, that the places we'll visit will remind me of something bigger than the fraught world inside my head. She tells me that if he knocks again, she'll be the one to go to the door. If I go and he says the wrong thing, I might react and our conflict could escalate.

I don't disagree with her.

I wake up in the middle of the night and sit up in bed with such suddenness that I disturb Denise.

"What is it?" she asks.

"I heard a phone ringing. It sounded to me like it was under the house."

"How could it be? There'd be no reception there. Were you asleep when you heard it?"

"I woke up hearing it too. I didn't dream the ring."

I roll out of bed, unsteady on my feet in the dark, and fumble into my pants, shirt, and slippers.

"What are you doing? The tunnel is in your head, Galen. Nothing's there."

Maybe not, but I see it as a mistake to underestimate the determination of our neighbor, our enemy. I walk to her side of the bed and drop down. I put my fingertips to the floor and listen.

"I don't feel anything here." I reach under the bed and grab my bat. "I'll check the rest of the house."

"I can't stand this anymore, Galen."

As I leave the bedroom, I'm thinking we'll need to cancel the trip. We don't want to leave the house vulnerable and return to find extensive damage or that the rooms have been emptied and our furniture replaced with theirs. Denise will say they wouldn't take it that far, but how can we know for sure what they'd do or try to do? We have rights, sure, but have they shown any respect for them? And how much good can our rights do us when we're not here to defend them?

I decide not to turn on any lights as I prowl. I check the front windows to see how many SUVs are parked along the curb, but I see only one in front of their house. I see no lights on in their house and backyard and hear no activity. The phone that rang has undoubtedly been turned off. I get down on all fours on the west side of the house, putting the bat aside but leaving it within reach. I don't feel vibrations beneath me or hear hacking, but I picture them underground, digging their way toward us and finally up. If someone's head pops through our floor, I hope he'll be the one leading the break-in. I'll pick up my bat and turn on a light. I'll let him get a look at what hit him.

POETRY

EDITED BY MAGGIE HESS

POETRY

HOLE REUNION SONNET

TANYA GRAE

for Courtney Love

Because the nineties are over. We grew up
& put away babydoll grunge & Mary Janes. Because
we heard "Violet" & our girl parts rumored with rage,
rant. Because we were not holes. Who *is* whole?
Our violence was inside. Because we played pretty,
played parts. Because there were holes only we could fill,
but couldn't see. Because good girls don't look for trouble,
but sometimes they do; sometimes it finds them. Because
we were more bad than good. Because the fairy tale lies
& who wants to act doe-eyed coy for some guy. Because
some part of me, maybe the missing part, awoke
on the spot. Because words like *slut* siren, that jaded knife.
I want to stay naked so you hear me. Because someone will
read this & think it's hot. Because hole must mean vagina.

TELL ME

SARAH JANCZAK

Where did he shove
all that Red?

Red of baby's bottoms, rust
Red   root Red

trigger Red. Red of teeth
just bitten into

flesh Red rotten
roasted   Red.

I dreamt you dead.
Not dying, not lying in bed

just straight up
heart stopped

dead. M, I can see you.
Your name   how it lingers

in the corner there   and again
always in his brightest Red.

Rodent Red   liquid Red
and torrid. Did you hide

in the walls with mice, M? Under
tables or umbrellas while it rained

Red? We are all golden
in our auras, M. We all seek

our sunset Red   poppy Red
the Red truth   of open mouths.

THOUGHTS ON A SUDDEN SPRING

CARRIE SHIPERS

According to the calendar, it's still
not spring, but overnight the air
has changed, made me think
of lighter sweaters and longer days,

less biting wind. It's hard to believe
it's really over, that I can put away
my boots and shovels, flannel
sheets and sidewalk salt. My dog

doesn't want his walks to end.
He whines when we turn onto
our block, again when I open the door.
Every day the grass seems greener,

and the trees have buds I think
must be new leaves. I'm worried
it's too soon, that one hard frost
will set us back. I even want to warn

the birds, already weaving
their new homes. If I'm going
to garden, I need to choose my seeds,
but I'm afraid to set my heart

on something growing, then wake
to still more snow. Maybe by May
I'll be convinced, and if not May,
then June for sure—I'll believe

in spring when summer comes,
when I've been warm for weeks.

FOR MY CREATIVE WRITING STUDENTS

DANTE DI STEFANO

For now, you coast on the cool grass of May
and think of the future only vaguely;
when you do, it is a mile wide and full
of stars. When you write it out, you call down
Andromeda and parse the clustered light,
but this is merely a kind of dreaming.
Sometimes the zodiac and its grace notes
stifle you as they wheel the air inside
your lungs. You love. You want to love. You break
desire into pulse and place two fingers
on a wrist, composing a heaven
from heartbeat and ache. You are still growing
into the wool of the self and the bruise
of your own stories. In unraveling
strangeness, you hold a drop of rain and call
it kindred. You can't look on linden trees
and glimpse the face of your dead, ghosting there.
However, the moon mothers you and skills
the edges of your winding sentences.
You find the necessary vowels stuck
in your throats and let them moan in the dark.
The need to say what you can't say unspools
itself from your mouths and hymnals a hope
as blue and speckled as a robin's egg.
When a song digs a dirge inside the wind

and you feel a grief catch you by the neck,
cup a prayer in your palms, hold both balled fists
out, and ask the world, ask God, ask sparrow
and field and clover and the holy green
waters unrolling at the confluence
of rivers, ask them to guess which hand it's in.

Haiku for Zainal Abidin, Martin Anderson, Andrew Chan, Rodrigo Gularte, Silvester Obiekwe Nwolise, Okwuduli Oyatanze, Raheem Agbaje Salami, and Myuran Sukumaran

Jenna Le

Say, how many men
does it take to shoot a mule?
In Jakarta: twelve

DAM S OF D   IC TION

Jenna Le

Fundamentals of Body CT: Third Edition by W. Richard Webb,
William E. Brant, and Nancy M. Major, p. 73

whi

    le

            form

      can compress the

        arteries or veins,

      The   sym-

metrical   pat   wit

      of the   ode   can be seen

      , indicating the benign nature

of the   process.

    b   u   t

      the right   time

is not   obvious   to

s   o   m   e   and

              calci-

fication does   occur.

BONDOJITO

ROSE HUNTER

you know in questions of memory and desire don't we often
get it wrong. friends.   whether they would be sea blue
or aquamarine or.   mother i have dead legs   deadpool
deadcushion dead, dead in the way on which are pinned your

hopes of something else.   in the waiting room clutching
        bulletproof envelopes of x-rays cts dopplers mris
like anxious job applicants and the children we always were.
        i know now we all come back around

and again just like this.   that mossy grenade
        i put it on the chest of drawers next to the television
in front of the cable box.   maybe it would ripen and then
we would know, what. but it only ever shrank and turned inwards
and gathered insects until it became a thud and a rolling rustle
        parceled with orange peels and moldy bread
bottom of the alley, past the three dogs.   when you're young

you don't know what they mean when they say *when you're young*.
        you think you do but you don't.   at bondojito

i left through those same doors you did. down   the stairs past the
turnstiles and men stretched out with covered faces under the eaves
the hum of electric lamps burning and wrinkling   the puddles
as i crossed eje 2 oriente, onto corzo to begin that walk home.

Central Library / W 5th St, Downtown LA

José Hernández Díaz

I went downtown to get books for the spring semester:

Codrescu, Ceravolo, Stein, Roberto Bolaño.

I placed my card on the clerk's desk.

"Do you still live at 220 Savanna Lane?"

"Mind your own business," I said.

"What's that?" he slid the card back.

"You need patience with novels,"

I retreated. "Everything is like that."

THE TULIPS

JUDITH SKILLMAN

How not liken them to lipsticks,
these varnished petals, Mars reds
set in a vase
on a granite countertop.

What of the abortion
my niece had earlier today
in Montreal, the Lamartine
to dilate her cervix?

Set a still life beneath a spotlight.
Light a gardenia-scented candle.
Let your breath blow it out.
Whisper at the altar of apology.

The yellow bucket carries secrets.
The purple holds sway,
and the latest, just-picked—
Alizarin, almost regal.

Recall that smack between the ribs
that knocks the wind out.
Come argument, come night-thoughts.
Remind youth of its soft skin,

age of its own disappearance.
Once a petal fell. Was it heard?
Did the rumble of carapace, kin
to locust, frighten anyone?

Bat Exclusion

Melody S. Gee

All August, our house drips
with bats' oily bodies
slung everywhere like leather fruit.
Our house a sudden orchard.

We learn there are young tucked above
the porch's bead board.
That where they are born

will echo all their lives.
No matter the shelter of southern caves
full of water-grazing insects,

our dim, exposed porch is forever
where these missiles home in.

I read that they can hang from
a scratch in a light bulb.
They can alight thin as a line.

Three men seal every crack around
escape tubes that prevent reentry.
The grease records silent exile.

The men say, expect the babies
to return for five seasons.

Shedding their winter caves
they will make a miniature
migration to city parks and rafters.

They will always find their first place,
but will move on when locked out.
Experience will finally tell them

abandon the empty echo, every call
returns the same knowledge;
you could wait for it, but don't.

♀

Daniel Aristi

What's now under your ice?

If the alimony

Is paid, will you rest

Till the spring?

(The men keep on dancing)

Example:

    Open halfway the kitchen drawer:

    Cutlery darts out backwards and, cling! halts;

    All these tails identical, but you know well

    —Forks to the left, spoons to the right, and knives in the middle.

    He'd always pulled them out in full to check their faces.

    Same thing with the children.

¿Qué hay ahora bajo tu hielo?

¿Si la pensión

Se paga, reposarás

Hasta la primavera?

(Los hombres continúan bailando)

Ejemplo:

    Abre hasta la mitad el cajón de la cocina:

    Los cubiertos salen fuera marcha atrás y ¡cling! se paran;

    Todas estas colas idénticas, pero tú sabes bien

    —Los tenedores a la izquierda, cucharas a la derecha, y cuchillos en la mitad.

    Él siempre los sacó fuera del todo para verles las caras.

    Lo mismo con los niños.

For Weeks, I Bore Those Bruises Like a Badge

M. Ann Hull

It's not the tragedies that kill us; it's the messes.
—Dorothy Parker

My summer sister was a different
sibling, her fingers stained sticky
with blackberry blood. We plucked
plush flesh, fresh from the bush, &
her grin was rich with grainy theft.
We raided ripeness to the teeth
& squished & squelched & squeezed
the kernels of sweet 'til our tongues
looked like we'd licked ink. These
were *our* small messes & our fingers
stained to the quick so quickly, we
lived like a laugh, in staccato ripples
of heat. That the berries weren't
ours, that the whole bush belonged
to a neighbor whose eyeholes would
blink & squint & shut behind blinds,
were facts we were coolly immune to,
bemused by. But when vines traded
their bitten beads for bitter blades
of icicles no one in their right minds
would savor, our friendship started
speaking through lips cracked dry &
split & we frequently left our doors
locked, rarely venturing outside. One
time, screeching home to meet her

as ungracefully as if I were wrestling
a snowflake to the ground, I slipped
hard & slid across the yard, cutting
deep both knees through the slicing
can opener of ice the world had become
overnight. I lay like a discarded beam
of light in a basement; she lit off,
yelling through the door at me for
weeping & wailing down the street until
my embarrassment echoed through
the neighborhood like a shutter-
slamming winter wind that won't die.
I went inside to face her screams
when her eyes fluttered like a dried
moth body & dropped to where
the blood puddled in my kneecaps &
the color painted me so many shades
of blue & gray I'll never be able
to name. I'll never bear bruises that way
again. My winter sister was a different
sibling entirely, but in that moment,
her eyes glittered & lips puckered
like she'd closed her mouth around
the bitterest berry, & she apologized
like she was praying to my knees.

33 LESSONS IN CAMOUFLAGE

MARTIN OTT

1

Mom switched me from southpaw
    to rightie, an abandonment of sorts,

    child on a basket of reeds adopted
by a land too scoured to hide beliefs.

2

As a boy, I read a fable of stacked
    turtles stretching to touch the sky,

    moral lost, just the teetering way
of latching onto the ladder upward.

3

A pigeon on the Hollywood Walk
    of Fame picks at a discarded fried

    chicken bag, cannibalism a lesson
of survival when scuttling on stars.

4

My ghost hand reasserts itself in odd
        ways, picking weeds, steering wheel,

        pleasing a lover, terrapin unshelled
when there is no one to drop you.

5

Interrogation was a nesting doll
        of camouflage, uniform as skin,

        questions as fists to pummel any
chance to unhinge the man within.

6

The checkered shirts in my office,
        flimsy remnants of boyhood flannel,

        hide the wolves and sheep in equal
measure, demand wrapped in leisure.

7

The coyote outside my window curls
        into the dirt, family scattered beneath

sloping canyon, the hunting reunions
enough to wake me even in daylight.

8

The melancholy house with an address
      ending in ½ displays a blue door, one per

      floor, opening to air, cerulean patches,
no clouds, inner tranquility or madness.

9

I lost my glasses once in a snow pile,
      too scared to tell my folks, sifting

      powder day by day until thaw, glad
for once they didn't notice my loss.

10

Good interrogators feel more not less;
      it's not nearly enough to wear a mask,

      eye mirrors projecting wish fulfillment,
ricochets inflicting collateral damage.

11

I once read a poem about a butchered
        goat and told myself that it was about

        the war, the ritualistic flaps and knife
sharpening, the earth soaked through.

12

Our gladiators have cameras on them.
        They strike in unexpected flurries.

        The stadiums vibrate with victory
chants. The ballet of the broken.

13

A couple in my neighborhood hangs
        chandeliers in trees, beacons to kids,

        the illumination of the outside path,
sorrows pushed onto the lawn.

14

One day, in a hurry, I felt an object
        in my shoe and discovered a button

from my shirt, remnants of a love
affair of objects behind my back.

15

We scrubbed the tracks of armored
      vehicles for hours after mud runs,

      separation of weapons and earth,
the union of men in boiling hours.

16

The world's most expensive coffee
      is sifted from poo, Jacu Bird brew,

      Black Ivory blend, civets force fed
plump beans, a filter of pit and rue.

17

My boss used to ask me to smile more,
      a daily dose of subservience, white

      gates opening, the lesson of keeping
enemies inside without swallowing.

18

In dead planets drifting in space,
     between solar freeze and magma

     core, life could coil
in countless oceans in the dark.

19

When my girlfriend takes a shower
     I stare at her silhouette through curtains,

     the outer sheath a filmy map of the world,
breath melting ice caps, my own thaw unseen.

20

The first person to nestle a baby
     in a cake, in any form, must have

     known bulges cannot be hidden,
that hunger is its own discovery.

21

We started a fire on the shooting range,
     beat the brush with ponchos to keep

the forest from engulfing us, tiny enemies
licking at our feet, the wildfires of war.

22

The state of being is not unlike
        the state of unbeing. The illnesses

        that writhe beneath the surface pull on us,
tiny passengers with unknown agendas.

23

The 25th hour is like an earring
        worn in an experimental phase,

        the past spilling from corduroy pockets,
once baggage in the uniformed me.

24

The older I get, the less well I do at hide
        and seek, my kids able to see the bulges

        poking out, fewer places for me to disappear,
the essence of fatherhood to be in plain view.

25

The pop star jokes how a girl who hid during
    the war would have been a screaming

    fan, his vanguard planning an invasion,
the truth of the man strewn in the message.

26

My daughter and I notice the missing letters
    on the pastry signage: *Do_uts* and the other

    homonymous messages of warnings, the truth
of LA visible not in beauty but the fading away.

27

There is a parasite in cats derived from rats that drives
    risky behavior. Nearly half the world's people

    have the urge, so many of our compulsions wired
and wrung, the path to our nature kinked and knotted.

28

When I was a boy I read the old and new testaments
    on my own and knew that God was a jealous

bully, the bible the word of men I did not
want to follow, faith in myself: divinity in strange places.

29

The past harmonizes, waiting for when
    we are most like our former selves, a symphony

    that thrums in foot tapping and humming,
the body a radio for ghosts we've forgotten.

30

I played army with the box of men kept alive
    in the attic, soldiers

    in battles with cowboys and dinosaurs,
an alien armada waiting, a man waiting.

31

We lose ourselves in books, in love making,
    in the crannies of our work and passions,

    the miscellany of the unrecorded world,
discovery of who we choose to master.

32

Not long ago we placed men in boxes, iced
        them, drowned them, for the idea of freedom.

        The measurement of pain is international.
Not long ago is idling down many roads.

33

I hide my strengths and weaknesses,
        clever boy, but my children expose

        them with their own. Each day a scab
is torn and each night a new me forms.

NONFICTION

EDITED BY ANN BEMAN

NON
FICT
ION

CONSEQUENCE OF COLORS: A BRIEF ESSAY IN KILLINGS

Michael Schmeltzer

I. THE CATERPILLAR

I WORE A black backpack, a spring jacket. Velcro shoes with the gray straps crossed. I left grade school with the quickstep of a young kid, my brown eyes cast down like roots.

I had no excuse. I had seen its green undulation, even stopped and squatted and stared. I stood and raised my foot then slammed it on the sidewalk. As if speed could prevent malice or intent. As if the caterpillar could offer resistance.

It was the first thing I remember killing.

I did not feel anger or repulsion or hate. It was the length of a toddler's finger and just as harmless. It was blurred with fuzz and in my path. It was curiosity gone callous.

When I raised my foot the color had dimmed and a distortion of its shape remained. Almost immediately I ran, as if rue—the warning within cruelty—wouldn't sting me, wouldn't follow me home.

II. THE FLIES

FROM ROOM TO room I killed them all, smashed them one by one against the windows. That summer, the flies arrived with the small drone of jaw harps. I crushed a half-dozen or so in minutes.

I remember the squashed black bodies against the light blue swatter. I remember the off-white of what I think were the guts. Within that mesh square, a storm of organs and oil-slick wings, some of them trembling.

There was nowhere to run; I was already home.

From that point forward, I refused to kill an insect if I could avoid it. I cup moths in my hands, trap spiders in a jar. Once, I held a bee on my palm while working the register at the grocery store. How odd it must have appeared, the bee like a lemon drop resting in one hand while the other hand scanned canned goods and cold cuts.

I don't know how else to say this; ultimately, it was the colors that convinced me not to harm another bug. The pepper flake of a gnat, the veined sunset of monarchs. Then there is the camouflage of a caterpillar smeared, the inside of flies like an infection of white. The only explanation I can offer is there are colors buzzing all around but some aren't meant to be seen.

Courage

Peter Grandbois

I want burning.
—Rumi

COURAGE CAN'T EXIST without knowledge. A man who doesn't know or understand the potential danger when he walks into a burning building to save a child doesn't exhibit courage. A soldier who enlists dreaming of video game warfare where he rescues his friends under sniper fire doesn't exhibit courage. He can't understand until he's lived through at least one battle, even then it's only a glimmer. Wait until he returns home and has to face the PTSD. The meaningless days piled one on top of another. A woman who has one child can't exhibit courage. She doesn't yet understand the nature of the pain. Going back for the second, that's courage.

I used to be fond of Rumi's quote. I once told a close friend in all seriousness, "I want burning," as if it was something you could ask for in a store. Something you could purchase. I thought it made me cool, someone who was at once passionate and willing to risk it all. I understand Rumi was talking about a relationship with God here, a relationship beyond words, beyond ritual, beyond the known. An ecstatic relationship in which you open yourself to the divine. I know his point is that mystics get burned. The divine exists outside the human, to go there you must forego the superficial trappings of bourgeois life, the life of the family man. Like the artist, you have to live outside the narrative and sometimes, as Paul Chaat Smith reminds us, "to be outside the narrative is not to exist."[1] To be outside the narrative, that takes real courage. Or insanity. Or both. There is no road map outside the narrative. Nowhere to go when the burning gets to be too much.

It's easy to say, "I want burning," when your life is going well. When your life fits the narrative you've written for it. I had a great job in academia. My books were getting published. My children appeared to be doing well. My marriage appeared to be doing well. The thing about fire is that it burns away appearances. To face the possibility of separation and divorce every day for three years. To have a child scream that she wants to die because the pain is too great, or that she hates you, or that she'll never forgive you because you cannot take away her pain. To stand before your child and know you can't do anything in the face of her mental illness, but to try to be there for her anyway. That's what it means to burn. To sit down with your wife and calmly discuss the terms of separation even though you both know you love each other, even though neither of you wants to separate, even though neither of you could ever in your wildest dreams imagine breaking up the family. That's what it means to burn. There is no narrative for these things.

I remember around 1989 or 1990, I was fencing a direct elimination bout in Kansas or Nebraska or New Mexico—the places have all blended into one. My opponent's blade broke as he attacked. As he lunged, the broken blade penetrated my leg. Not much. More of a scratch really. A flesh wound, for the Monty Python fans out there. But it bled a lot. The blood soaked my entire thigh red before they could stop the bleeding. After a short injury time-out, I was ready to fence. I couldn't move my leg well, but it didn't hurt. My opponent looked pale as he returned to the strip. He couldn't muster the courage to attack me, or if he did, his attacks were feeble, and I easily parried them, then launched my own. It took more courage for my opponent to face my blood-stained leg than it did for me to fence with it. The beauty of youth is that I had no idea I could have hurt myself further.

As a veteran fencer, a fencer over fifty, it's a whole different world. Every time I go to practice. Every time I get on the strip at a tournament, I know very well what I could do to myself. My body doesn't let me forget. The tendinitis in my hand and wrist and elbow, the shooting pain in my lower back and hip, the sharp pain in my right knee, the arthritis in my left foot, remind me with each step that if I make a wrong move, I will not be the same person I was yesterday. Every morning after fencing when I rise from bed, I face the fact that I may have crippling arthritis in another ten or fifteen years. I feel it in my bones, and yet I keep fencing. Why? Why continue to fence when I know what it will do to my body? Is that courage? Stupidity? We think courage is an attribute of youth, but the young haven't the foggiest idea what the word means. You have to live a little to understand what you can lose.

A man who is not on fire is nothing.
—Carl Jung

I used to think life was about achievement. I used to mark my life by the goals I'd set myself. There's something about youth that wants, no needs, to be on the move, to keep running. As a young man, I was terrified of being seen as "normal," of fitting into the narrative. And so I fenced. I excelled in medieval literature and the Old English language. I prided myself on being anachronistic. Being different. Even now I've carefully cultivated my narrative to always exist on the outside. I read international literature and books from independent publishers. Never mainstream American fiction—whatever that is. I write books for small presses, books the corporate publishing houses would scoff at because in the words of so many of my rejection slips: "We don't know how to position this." I review primarily small press books for magazines, who, in turn, primarily publish reviews of small press books. I am the champion of the fringe.

Books are dangerous. That's why they get burned. That's what sets them apart. Books, real books, not the kind that can be made into movies or videogames, are the closest we can get to entering the consciousness of another, to having empathy. Real empathy. Virginia Woolf's *To the Lighthouse* kind of empathy, José Donoso's *The Obscene Bird of Night* kind of empathy, David Markson's *Wittgenstein's Mistress*, Ann Quin's *Berg*, Percival Everett's *Erasure*, William Faulkner's *As I Lay Dying*. These books cannot be made into movies, despite James Franco's megalomaniacal attempts to do so. These books use the alchemy of language and point of view to bring us inside the consciousness of another. Movies can't do that. Video games can't do that. They do plot. They do special effects. They do beautiful faces projected on a giant screen. They do these things really well. Books with a capital "B" understand the power of the word. They know that a well-crafted sentence can also burn. The right word can sear itself into flesh, the way the single word shift in point of view in Hemingway's "Hills Like White Elephants" transforms the story and therefore us—"They were all waiting *reasonably* for the train." A paragraph honed to perfection can work its way inside so deeply there's no possibility of excision. It lingers and hurts like a lost love.

> *What matters most is how well you walk through the fire.*
> —Bukowski

Last night I fenced the bronze medalist from the 2004 Olympics in Athens. He visited our club in Columbus, and he kicked my ass. I asked if I could fence him again. Again, he killed me. I asked him to fence one more time. He toyed with me. I could do nothing. I would have fenced him again, but I needed to get my daughter home, who at this point was thoroughly embarrassed watching her father willingly return again and again to the seat of humiliation. I left the club exhilarated, more alive than I'd felt in a long time. No matter the fact that my elbow throbbed so much I couldn't pick up my water bottle after. My daughter laughed at me on the car ride home. "You'd fence until you dropped," she said. And she was right. It wasn't about wanting to win. Forget the tendinitis in my elbow. He was twenty years younger than me. He hadn't stopped training for seventeen years as I had. Even if I'd never stopped fencing and was magically made younger, this Olympic bronze medalist was a far better fencer than I'd ever been. It was about the dance. It was about the need to burn. It's good to get your ass kicked. Even better to get it kicked again and again no matter how hard you try.

Recently, I fenced in a local tournament in Columbus. Because it was "an open" it meant that I'd fence against men and women ranging in age from ten to seventy-five. One woman there could not have been a day younger than seventy. She wasn't in my pool, but she caught my attention, nonetheless. Decked out in full regalia, it was clear she'd made a significant investment in fencing. It was also clear she knew what she was doing. Her basic form was good. She understood the actions. She must have fenced for a good portion of her long life. I watched her fence her first bout. She lost five to zero. After, she shook hands with her opponent, unhooked, and calmly sat down. Ten minutes later, they called her to strip for her next bout. Again, she lost five to zero. She didn't score a touch all day. Yet, every time they called her to strip, she walked over, hooked up, saluted her opponent and donned her mask. It was only in the last instant, as her mask went down, that I spotted in the cold set of her eyes something all fencers understand. The determination to fight. It is how we recognize each other. It was not a game for her. It was not an easy way to pass the time, the way so many seniors use golf or tennis. She didn't smile. Her face held only the look of calm determination. And yet she had no hope of scoring even a touch. That's courage. That's what it means to burn in sport.

It isn't much different for the artist. I have measured out my life in rejection slips, to steal a line from Eliot. Sometimes when I tell my students that my novels have been rejected forty or fifty times, that some stories have been rejected seventy, eighty plus times, when I tell them my most recent novel took four years to write, and I've now been sending it out and having it rejected for three years, I see looks of abject horror. Then, just to kick them over the edge, I let them know that even if it does get published, it will most likely sell no more than a thousand copies. I might make a thousand dollars, if I'm lucky. *Why do it?* they ask, unable to fathom a process where "success" takes so long and is so difficult to measure, at least with metrics that fit the narrative, or where success may not happen at all. *Why submit yourself to such a bleak process?* they ask, and I tell them if they have to ask the question, they may already have their answer.

The rise of the Internet and computer software that makes independent publishing affordable has transformed the publishing landscape over the last thirty years. Many of the best books now come from small, independent presses. And yet, so few get read. Fewer still win prizes. Books from independent presses make up about two percent of the finalists in fiction for the Pulitzer, the National Book Award, and the National Book Critics Circle Award over the last thirty years. You don't believe me? Run a check. I did. Rarely, if ever, is one of those books reviewed in the major papers. There is very, very little courage in the mainstream publishing industry. And newspapers? Well, they're going the way of the dinosaurs.

Still, small presses keep emerging. They keep growing. Somehow, the books find their way into the hands of readers who press them to their lips, knowing full well the price of immolation.

What is to give light, must endure burning.
—Viktor Frankl

We don't choose to burn. We don't choose when to show courage. That was my mistake in telling my friend that I wanted burning. My hubris. I had no idea what was in store for me. Had I known, I would never have said those words, never have chosen to burn. The narrative we are sold says we can control our lives. It says we can have the house with the white picket fence, marry the woman we'll love for the rest of our lives, have two and a half children who will grow up to be happy and healthy and to do it all again. It says, play by the rules, try hard, set your mind to it, and you can have it all. It's all about positive thinking, knowing what you want, imagining it, and it will be so. But it turns out that's all an illusion designed to keep comfortable consumers. To quote Leonard Cohen, "You live your life as if it's real." When it turns out that life is about as far from that "reality" as we can imagine, that life is much messier than we've been told, many of us retreat to our addictions of choice.

Unless we don't. Unless we refuse. Allow ourselves to burn. Two years ago, I almost left my marriage. My family. Even now, two years later, it's sometimes a fight to stay in it. Some days are good. Other days, I feel as if I will break, as if I'm already broken. On those days, it's as if the next word spoken, the next sound will shatter me. My wife and I work really hard at our marriage. With three kids, and each of us in a career, it's difficult to find the time to talk. Or at least time when we're not both exhausted. When we do talk, things can go south pretty fast. It used to scare me. It used to scare me so much that I would avoid talking at any cost. I would isolate myself. Find things to do. It's easy when you're a teacher. There are always more papers to grade, lessons to plan, things to read. It's easy when you have three kids. One of them always needs your attention. It's easy when you have as many passions as I do. I can slip into fencing, writing, reading, painting, music, and never have to face the fire.

But then I started fencing again at the veterans level. I remember walking on the strip those first few tournaments and telling myself I was the best fencer in the room, that I could beat anyone. And I remember a little voice answered back. Yeah, but now any one of them can also beat you. Things are different in the veterans. It doesn't all boil down to skill, or tactics, or tenacity. It doesn't come down to who has the killer instinct, as it so often did when I was younger. In the veterans, you become painfully aware that no matter how good your technique or how strong your killer instinct, your body can fail you at any moment. You often think of the right tactical move, but your body refuses to carry it out. We are all plagued by injury, pains that affect the outcome in what often seem arbitrary ways. We, each of us, come to the strip carrying a lifetime of emotional baggage that shapes the bout. When you're young, all you want to do is win. When you're older, yes you want to win, but you also know that your opponent may have just lost his father, or that he is having trouble with one of his children. You know because you sat with him, talking about it over a bourbon the night before. You know, too, that your own worries over your children make it difficult to concentrate on this day. All of these things make winning in the veterans division seem arbitrary at best and downright capricious at worst.

It was a frightening realization to know how easy it was to lose to "lesser" fencers in the veterans. Then, almost as quickly, it wasn't. It became liberating. I realized if I didn't have to worry about losing, if it's so arbitrary, I didn't have to worry about winning. I was free to dance. Some dances are beautiful. Some brutal. But the outcome was no longer important. All that mattered was doing it. And isn't that life? Isn't that what relationships are all about?

The definition of a successful marriage is being willing to live in a mess. I don't mean a physical mess. I'm not talking about a pigsty. I'm talking about an emotional mess. I'm talking about being willing to lose, acknowledging that on a daily basis you will lose as much as, or more than, you win. We have a lot of narratives of control in this country. Our entire national narrative is built on the "fact" that we are the best, that we will always be the best, that we can never lose. We are so sure that if we follow the rules, if we just do things a certain way, we will achieve success. We will be happy. We will win. But it's simply not true.

Recently, my wife and I sat out on the back deck. It was a clear night with so many stars. The kids were inside: one doing homework, the other on her cellphone, the other watching TV. It was past their bedtime, but we decided to let go of the rules for this night. We needed to talk.

"Is it time for us to separate?" I asked. "Time for us to move on?" As if there could be an answer. I didn't look at my wife but stared up into the bowl of stars.

"I don't feel like I have a husband," she said. It wasn't an attack. Her flat tone suggested just how tired we each were of the pain we continued to inflict on each other. The ways in which each had failed to support the other.

"I don't feel like I have a wife," I responded, perhaps too quickly, wanting to be sure we started the conversation on the same footing. "We seem to bring each other down."

My wife took a deep breath, and we sat in silence for what seemed like a long time. "So, what's the worst that can happen?" she asked. "We move to different houses. Shuttle the kids back and forth. Deal with the traumas that follow."

"Yep," I said, still not turning toward her. "We could even live across the street from each other. It wouldn't be that bad."

"Not really any worse than being together," she replied. And this time, she turned toward me and smiled.

I reached out for her hand. Her smile always did that to me. Took me straight back to those first few times we went out, when I'd catch her smiling at me from across the table. "I guess the world won't come to an end, either way," I said, and we both laughed.

"The kids would be okay."

"Eventually."

"Yes," she said. "Eventually."

"Look at that," I said, letting go of her hand to point toward the eastern horizon. "Look how bright those two stars are. Do you suppose they're planets?"

"That one on the left is probably Venus," my wife said.

"Maybe the one on the right is Jupiter."

"Maybe."

"It's strange that they're both so bright," I said.

We sat like that for a long time, neither of us saying anything more until our youngest joined us, saying he was ready for bed. I squatted down for him to climb on my back as had become our habit, then couldn't help but point out the two planets. "Mom thinks that one's Venus and the other one's Jupiter," I said. "If you were an astronaut, which one would you rather visit?"

"I don't care," he said, sleepily. "Venus is hot, and you'd sink through the gases of Jupiter. They'd both be hard places to live."

As usual, my wife fell asleep in our son's bed, and I fell asleep in our daughter's. Only much later in the night did we find our way back to our own, but by then we were too tired to talk. I have trouble sleeping, and so I stared out the window. I'd heard that when NASA plots a course for a mission to the moon or Mars it's not a straight line, but a series of corrections and mis-corrections, like a sailboat tacking upwind. I wondered about that jagged path. I wondered how long it would take to arrive.

NOTES

1. Smith, Paul Chaat, *Everything You Know About Indians is Wrong* (Minneapolis: University of Minnesota Press, 2009), p. 51.

WINDOW

KRISTEN NICHOLS

THE NEWS COMES as it does with this kind of thing. One friend asks about another, a lost friend who has seasons where she disappears, and the one friend shares news of the ex-husband, of pancreatic cancer and the dark prognosis.

And the people, they aren't part of your life anymore, although she—the lost friend—once was. You remember that day you walked to the back of that new church with your brand new baby, and there she was, that beautiful bright blonde woman with the blonde little boys and the beaming smile and the friendly heart and the grace to reach out her hand to be your very first friend in a brand new town.

For a season you did life alongside this family. Her husband, the photographer, was good at witty banter with your husband. They had a beer once in awhile. She was a sharp, hilarious, young mom who encouraged you to get out of yourself and not be so scared all the time, to steady your shaky mom-feet and go to the play dates and drink coffee and wine and laugh at just trying to survive the first wonderful-awful days of loving your kids. She talked to her boys with patience and wisdom. You marveled at her quiet voice and the way she knew just the right words for them. You tried to have the same with your daughter and failed, day after day.

Her husband took your pictures, first of your round pregnant belly full of boy-child and then of that boy and his sister and his daddy later on. They are beautiful shots, your husband in his firefighter turnouts, staring up at the camera with the eyes you fell in love with. Your kids, messy-haired and dressed in play clothes a bit too small, as if even in that still moment on film they are changing.

You will remember his exhibition at the gallery downtown, that photo shoot of their babysitter in a white dress and the way she jumped right into the water when he asked her to. Somehow he shot the photos from underneath, the white dress flowing out and up and around her, her dark hair fanning out in the water.

The lost friend eventually told you about the anger and his affairs. About the details he left out when they first met. His HIV-positive ex-wife. The girlfriend he met in Thailand when he was sent there on photo assignment. His thing was Asian women, and once you know that you look differently at his photos, the women and the graceful turns of their necks, their eyes, their lips and lowered lashes. He liked young girls too, she said, which you already know because she was seventeen and he was in his mid-thirties when they met. Then one day she came and sat in your backyard, dark-eyed, overweight, and telling you about the night he got so angry with her she collapsed and someone called 911. Your husband said he wished he could wash the house free of her darkness after she left. Maybe a year later you saw her and called to her in the CVS parking lot one night, almost ran to her and hugged her too tight. Her eyes said she wanted to escape. You knew it wasn't you she was running from.

You will think of her often when you drive up the parkway, the way you used to go to her house. You've heard that she has an artsy, cab-driving young boyfriend, a man closer to her age, and it won't surprise you when she marries him.

She has reappeared now and then on social media—you're used to being friended and unfriended. When you can see them, you'll see by the pictures that she has made things amicable with him, the ex-husband photographer. Their boys stand next to his hospital bed, their eyes unlit and faces wrapped in sad smiles. His cheeks are sunken but oddly red, his smile the same as it ever was, completely masking what was happening beneath it. The only window to that man was through his camera. He dies only days after that last picture.

She posts something beautiful that makes you cry. Something about how no matter what happened between them, he was her first love and gave her the best gifts, those three boys. And with that, it ends.

The mortuary is next to the freeway, and you drive by on the day of his funeral. You are driving your kids to school, and you notice the hearse in front of the building.

You'll sit there in the driver's seat, the chirp of your children and the positive hits radio station playing and you'll marvel at the passage of the moments. At the change. At the speed. The sky rises above you between the rocky hills ahead, blue, clear and clean.

COTTON FRAMES

ALLISON COFFELT

LOUNA JULIEN HUMS as she works, her forty-year-old fingers turn pages searching for the sheet she needs, her shoulders back and spine straight. The box she holds is as big as a piece of paper and three inches deep. It is full of notes and little orange packets of serum for people to mix with water in case of a diarrhea emergency. On top of the box rests a green plastic envelope for if—no, for *when*—the skies open up and fat drops start to fall. It is rainy season in Haiti.

Louna is maybe 5'3", the shorter side of many Haitian women I have met. She doesn't quite reach my shoulders. Her muscular legs and arms accompany a rounder belly and chest, and her graying hair is mostly covered by her cap. A few staccatos of silver and black hair jutt under her jaw. When she listens, her eyes tune in from imploring to discerning.

Today we are working in Louna's community. Louna's neighborhood. People listen and greet her and she knows everyone's name. We are talking about sanitation, clean water, family planning, and the services at Maison de Naissance.

It is not really we. She is talking; I am tagging along. Watching. Maison de Naissance, or MN, is a birthing home in southern rural Haiti in the province of Larnage. Les Cayes, one of the bigger cities in the South, is where I'm staying. Each day, I hitch a ride with the other *blan,* or white foreigner, one or two of the nurses, and the sanitation team in MN's white Range Rover. There are two identical cars: one always stays at MN as an ambulance, and the other brings shifts of workers back and forth from the city.

I first learned about MN in college. My interest in Haiti had begun a few years before (predictably, with a book) and when I found out about a group on my campus that partnered with what they called a "grassroots nonprofit" in southern Haiti, I was reluctant to get involved. I'd read enough horror stories of helping gone wrong (think suitcase medicine where you bring what's needed and leave without any real change) to think I knew better. I knew things were complex, but I didn't know the complexity of the complex. I'm still learning that.

How messy things can be and, in the same glance, beautiful and hopeful and good and, really, especially, how much I don't know.

To get to MN, we scoot between lanes, around a roundabout, zip by vendors, brake for passing cars, turn right, and jostle down gravel for another twenty minutes. I do not know what it means to jostle until I take this route. This road isn't gravel. It's just dirt with a few rocks. We begin to pass cows, shacks, and plots of land. We're closer. MN is in the sticks.

Louna inhales deeply, rocks back, leans forward. Big sigh. She settles into her seated posture. She is done joking with the kids and mothers. There'll be laughter again later. She pauses for a moment.

"Now," she begins. "Do you know about the services of Maison de Naissance? Tell me."

Or,

"Do you know how to keep your water clean? Tell me how you clean your water."

She is a nurse and neighbor; they readily respond. They talk about how they keep their home and pots clean, how they sanitize their water, and how they wash their hands. They ask about the ratio of container size to water sanitation pills.

A woman goes and gets her bucket.

"How many pills would I use with this?"

Louna rests her hand on her mouth.

Louna is a Community Health Worker or Health Promoter and her responsibility is door-to-door visits. As she talks, she draws parallels. The water treatment takes half an hour. One woman asks how to measure thirty minutes without a watch. Louna says to "wait for a good moment. It's the time you can walk from here to the road." The woman asks another question.

"One pill," Louna says, "will clean three small bottles, the size of Coca-Cola."

A grin begins to awake from its nap beneath Louna's lips, stretching out slowly. She shifts back to community-friend Louna, and her laughter rises, a crescendo from her gut moving up until it is almost a giggle, as earnest as a giggle, but still so jolly, singing high and low notes. She shakes her head underneath the black ball cap that reads *FL* on the front and *Florida* on the back Velcro under her twist-ponytail.

When the mother or father isn't home and Louna isn't offered a chair, she uses her box to write, bracing it between her hip and a tree. She makes a note to come back. Her chart details the person she spoke with, what about, and recommendations she made. Silhouette from afar: a short, round woman propping up a little box in the shadow of a tall, skinny palm tree.

• • •

Haiti is a graveyard for clothes.

From somewhere I recalled generic images of African women in vivid oranges and reds, head wraps of majestic purple, carrying pitchers of water on their crowns. I knew enough to know it wouldn't look like a movie, but the stories we carry are hard to shake. An artist friend once told me about a theory where class and a society's "development" are reflected in color. The crux was that women in poorer countries tended to embrace patterns, bold colors, and bright hues more than women in richer countries. The women in richer countries, apparently, prefer subtle shades and neutrals. I can't find this theory anywhere when I look. But I notice this: I don't own many bright colors.

There were in fact pitchers of water to be carried in Haiti. And baskets of bread, chairs, tables—all meticulously, beautifully balanced atop a woman's head. And sometimes on a motorbike after that. But I saw no long, flowing, original clothing, no bolts of vibrant fabric in the markets. I saw t-shirts.

There were also dresses, old labels, new labels, pants, skirts, shorts. Imagine a Goodwill fashion show.

Between 1990 and 2003, seven billion pounds of used textiles were exported from America to other countries. This is what Pietra Rivoli reports in her book *Travels of a T-Shirt in a Global Economy*. They are purchased by companies like the Trans-Americas Trading Company, which sorts, packages, ships, and sells huge bundles of clothing to places like Haiti.

That's enough clothing to rock an economy and a culture. Enough to change the language. A whole vocabulary sprung up. In Tanzania, these imported cast-offs are called *mitumba*. In Zambia, the word is *salaula*. In Bolivia: *ropa usada*. It's *pèpè* in Haiti.

I wonder where the cold-weather clothes go.

While the slogan of Trans-Americas Trading Company is *recycling textiles since 1942,* I doubt the green-ness of packing 54,000 pounds of clothing into each forty-foot High Cube Container and shipping it halfway across the world. When I arrive at the company's website, the page automatically plays Muzak, making me question how up to date they keep their process and technology. Flooding far-off markets doesn't sound like recycling; someone must be making money.

I meet Nancie Wayack at Maison de Naissance while she waits for her pregnant friend to finish her appointment. Nancie is a merchant. Like everyone I've met here, she tries to sell enough to cover her children's school fees. I ask her what she sells.

"Clothes and food."

"Where do you get the clothes?"

"I bought them at Miragoâne."

"Miragoâne," says my translator Rozambert, "is a big commercial city where people can find the goods they need. It is more than ninety kilometers from where we are outside Les Cayes."

"How do you get the clothes from Miragoâne to here?"

"I pay a car to transport the clothes," Nancie says. "When I arrive at the city, I pay for transport."

"Do you get to choose the clothes you sell yourself?"

"No."

•••

I spent a decade circling back to Haiti. The feeling of wonder and intrigue that comes upon finding something that both captivates and teaches. The feeling of waking up. Later I would read *Bluets* by Maggie Nelson, and I felt I understood her when she wrote, "One of the men asks, '*Why blue?*' People ask me this question often. I never know how to respond. We don't get to choose what or whom we love, I want to say. We just don't get to choose." It was Haiti for me. I can trace it back; it was what Haiti taught me: first about myself, then about the world around me, and then about the collective "we" and the order of our priorities and systems.

I kept circling back mentally, never physically. I watched as people I knew went next door on Hispañola to the Dominican Republic. They went "down" to Mexico and El Salvador for church groups and alternative spring breaks. The trips dug a well of questions. Were these groups just bringing down supplies, feeling good about themselves, and then returning home, leaving the community relatively unchanged, waiting for the next delivery? Were they building houses or structures that could have been built by someone local? What if they had just donated what their trip cost to a group that was established and permanent? I was fifteen, sixteen, seventeen, too good and righteous and opinionated to take a poverty tourism trip.

I was eighteen, nineteen, twenty, in college with ideas and principles about aid and development. I was twenty-one and graduated. I was twenty-one and thinking about going to Haiti. I was twenty-one and broke. I went to California instead, to work at a student-based global health advocacy group where my co-worker kept a quote by her desk: "What I tell my students all the time is, you speak English, you have a passport, you have a responsibility to use those tools. Go see these places and talk about them. Write about them. Be an advocate. It's a huge job, but the coolest thing ever is to change the world."

The words were from Joia Mukherjee, Chief Medical Officer of Partners in Health, an organization I'd long respected for their approach to health as comprehensive. My thoughts on privilege, responsibility and bearing witness simmered; Joia's words beckoned me to keep thinking about traveling and writing— two longings I'd ignored because coming up with "why not" was easier than coming up with a plan.

• • •

That Saturday, we go to the market early. Merchants are getting ready. They set their goods out on their tarps carefully, like fine china on a tablecloth. A woman unpacks shoes as the sun climbs the sky. Dozens of rubbery black ballet flats that look new, all unused and all imported, that must not have sold first life. I'm guessing a place like Target rolled over a new season's clothes and couldn't have given them to a local Goodwill without undercutting their own market, so a company like Trans-Americas Trading enters the picture. The company can buy them from the supplier for cheap, take them far away, and sell them to poor people who sell them to other poor people. No wonder I don't see any Haitian seamstresses, tailors, or cobblers.

To sew clothing from a pattern, first you cut out the shape you need. Pin and tuck, cut and stitch until you construct the piece. The scraps of the pattern, if you hold them up to the light, highlight an absence; borders hang around a hole. With scraps, we see what exists by observing what is left.

On the way to the market, I ask Mackenzie, the friend who took us, how the clothes got here. I tell him about Nancie, who buys them from suppliers in loads.

"Where do they come from before that?" I ask.

"Now *that's* the question you have to be asking." He turns around from the front to look at me.

"Where *do* they come from before that?" Mackenzie repeats. He wears a white polo shirt with the crest of a prep school and a name like "North Valley" stitched in English. Before he moved to Les Cayes, he worked as a translator in Port-au-Prince where he met his wife, Kirsty, who is now the Clinical Director of MN. Mackenzie's English is excellent. His French is better. He and Kirsty speak Creole to their son.

"Many charities, church charities, and others in the United States collect clothes that people are no longer using," he says.

There are big merchants and businessmen, he explains, who have the access and ability to travel to the US. They have the green cards, the paperwork, and the customs connections to move merchandise. When they're in the US, they buy huge shipments of clothes from vendors. The clothes come tightly packed and measured by weight. They bring the clothes to a warehouse in Port-au-Prince, the South, or the North where workers break down bales.

The merchants sell the packages to women like Nancie. Nancie scrapes money together to buy the clothes, pays the car to drive her, and sets up a stall when she returns. Then she tries to sell enough clothes to cover her costs *and* pay for her children's school fees because she lives in a country where, even if the public schools and current population were spread evenly, there would be over 26,000 potential students for each public school. Haiti has an estimated four million people under the age of fifteen and fewer than 1,500 public primary schools. For many, private religious schools are the only viable option.

Nancie and her t-shirts are at the bottom of the food chain. The rules governing the t-shirt and cotton trade are highly specific and closely lobbied.

"T-shirts made from Caribbean-made fabric using US-made yarn may enter the United States freely, but only to a limit of 5,651,520 dozen in 2003."

That sentence comes from a section in Rivoli's book on the 2002 US-Caribbean Trade Partnership act.

Note the detail.

5,651,520 dozen?

5,651,520 dozen is the maximum t-shirt output of Fruit of the Loom factories in the US. If a Caribbean manufacturing plant imported more shirts than that, the market could be flooded, driving down prices.

These are the rules: no foreign yarn, only US-made; the yarn may be shipped to the Caribbean; the yarn must be made into cloth in the Caribbean because you can pay people with fewer rights less money; the cloth may or may not be made into t-shirts in the Caribbean; if the cloth is made of US yarn (not the whole shirt), and shipped back to the US it might qualify as MADE IN THE USA. The final product, the eventual t-shirt, is sold in the US to make US companies money.

• • •

Lingering on my hands today in Haiti is the smell of garlic. It's like when I cook at home. The scent hangs on my skin after a cool shower, bug spray, and many washes. The other *blan*, Emilie, and I had wanted to learn more about Haitian cooking and asked to help with dinner last night. For a few days, Emilie has been hanging around in the kitchen doorway of the medical compound where we're staying, chatting in French with the head cook. When we join them in the kitchen, I'm quiet. It doesn't matter what language you cut cilantro in. Here, muteness is a just little less apparent. As our fingers dance with the knives, I think about writer Edwidge Danticat:

You have always had your ten fingers. They curse you each time you force them around the contours of a pen. No, women like you don't write. They carve onion sculptures and potato statues. They sit in dark corners and braid their hair in new shapes and twists in order to control the stiffness, the unruliness, the rebelliousness.

What do the two women who cook do when they're not in the kitchen? The head cook lives in an upstairs room of the compound, but the younger woman, who usually makes the trips to the market, walks to work every day from somewhere else.

Our first few evenings, the head cook made what she thought Americans would want: casseroles. But what we wanted were rice and beans: Haitian food. As we cook together, we communicate. A couple days later we enjoy a traditional Haitian menu. We lick our fingers to a feast of fried plantains, fried breadfruit, fried potatoes with a touch of ketchup, rice, bean sauce, tomato wedges atop iceberg lettuce, and, of course, *pikliz*, a cabbage-based Haitian classic. We roll the two women compliment after compliment.

In the kitchen, yellow light from a few windows and an overhead absorbs the cooking figures while a fish the length of my forearm rests in a bucket under the sink. A pan will sizzle vegetable oil soon, and two dull knives, one small and one big, will go to work on everything. The refrigerator is full of plastic bags from the market. They aren't clear and thin, uniformly stamped with the word FRESH or PRODUCE like in supermarkets back home, but a mismatched rainbow of reused sacks.

How to crush garlic with a mortar and pestle: drop in one fresh bulb to grind. The younger cook demonstrates. Now your turn. A big chip of garlic pops up and arcs out, landing on the countertop. Grab it and toss it back in. Cooking is about working with pieces, trying things here and there, one way or another, and doing it again. Growing up is a messy process; it's searching through the cabinets to find ingredients, experiences, lessons, memories, and guring out what to set aside and what to mix in with who you are. Of course it all of it is always there. The kitchen countertop of my childhood was blue tiles embedded in dark grout. Here I find the same tiles, but orange. Run your hand over the uneven surface and feel the stone crumbs, working themselves out. Sweep them over the edge.

• • •

On weekday evenings when we drive back from MN, we pass houses with eight-foot high concrete walls out front. In the lane between these walls and the road, commerce hums—"free" enterprise. We pass carts selling cold Coca-Colas and Fruit Champagne sodas, endless shacks of lottery tickets, huts where you can buy everything from barrettes to crackers and packaged cookies to soccer balls. There are food stands where the deep fryer is smacking hot and the plantains and breadfruit will be dunked on your order. The sign painted in white on the wall of a salmon-pink convenience store advertises all the basics: spaghetti, bread, rice. Starch is cheap. There's a stand for tarps, many stamped with USAID, draped over a clothesline. Someone will buy and reuse one as a mat for their goods at market.

Then of course there are clothes stands. Every third station, we pass the merchants with clothes hung up along the tall walls. We zip by a prom dress or two, stiff pink ruffles or shiny maroon rayon, but mostly it's t-shirts and polos, cotton dresses and tank tops.

We drove by a man in one small town whose t-shirt requested somebody *Save Senior Week*. The shirt that reads PATRIOTS HOMECOMING has more meanings than I can bear. Walking around later, I see the same *D.A.R.E.* anti-drug t-shirt I had in fifth grade. Its diagonal red scrawl on light heather gray reminded me to *just say no*.

•••

Leaving MN and Les Cayes and heading North, the Haitian doctor I'm riding with, Marius Gardy, and I survey the roadside fruit stands. Fruit in the city can't compare to fruit from the countryside—in cost or quality. In the mountains the fruit is juicy, fresh, and not long off its vine. We come up on a fruit stand and slow down, Gardy eyeing the bowls, and accelerate again. We pass merchants on the side of the road without more than a second glance. I'm not sure what he's looking for. As we climb a green mountain, Gardy sees several women together on the side of the road and pulls over.

The women gather their fruit bowls—as much as they can carry—from under their tarp canopies and rush to the car. Gardy leaves it idling and hops out, walking around back to meet them. He teases the women and they protest back, banter bouncing between them. He coaxes them sweetly about the price: *oh no, no, no, cherie*. He told me later that he loves the barter, the haggle, but that he always wants to pay a fair price. By now we've moved on to evaluate the fruit. Pineapple? Yes, we want some pineapple. He picks up something else.

"Here, let me try," Gardy says.

He takes out his pocketknife and peels back the light green skin of a small ball.

"Have you tried this before? It's an orange."

He laughs at my expression—it peels like an orange and the inside is meaty with little pulp nodules, but it's not orange. He cuts off a chunk. The taste isn't quite as sour as a lemon.

We buy oranges. We get some cherries, too, which are almost green on the outside, and I pop one in my mouth.

"What do you think?" Gardy asks. He smiles at my sour face. "It's not something you'd just eat for a snack."

"It's a cherry, so I thought I knew."

"It's not like the cherries in the US. These are for juice. Do you know how to make the juice?"

I don't know, but later I drink some. Juice in Haiti is such a treat; it's the freshest of fruits and sugar—probably cane sugar—blended together. The juice I have is thick and pulpy with bits of the real fruit still hanging in the mix. We buy some cantaloupe and starfruit and a few other things. Gardy buys from all of the women. We load the fruit into the back of his Land Rover, next to my bag and the long, raw, sugar cane sticks that Gardy's mother gave him when he visited her in Les Cayes. I'd see people in markets working these sweet canes, carving into them, and selling off the wet, white meat in little shards. You chew on them. The fruit in the back gets loose and I offer to climb back and secure it.

"Don't worry about it. Don't worry, don't worry," he tells me. "They're just going for a ride. But they're not going anywhere. They can't get out."

We spend the rest of the car ride talking while melons and oranges roll like pinballs between sugar cane lanes and duffels of supplies.

• • •

I am sitting on a bench by a mangy dog sitting on an old desk chair. It is humid. I know humid. I live in the Midwest.

The damp leaves next to me glow from a sun so bright I squint, eyes stinging, across the gravel driveway, to hear the soft clinks of pans through the kitchen screen door. This morning I'm reading Anne Lamott:

> Writing involves seeing people suffer and, as Robert Stone once put it, finding some meaning therein. But you can't do that if you're not respectful. If you look at people and just see sloppy clothes or rich clothes, you're going to get them wrong.

Her words make me think about traps. She's asking for an acknowledgment of the obvious and the choice we can make to look closer. Seeing, really seeing, asks us to look beyond what we think we'll see or what we want to see and to simply observe. I'm still searching for the "meaning therein." One pattern I continue to find is respect. I see it in the doctors and the cooks in the compound where MN visitors rent rooms. I see it in Gardy when we talk about the function and role of aid in his country. It's why he started his own clinic. To

find the meaning therein, I ask what's common. In Haiti there's a saying: *tout moun se moun.*
Every person is a person.

That old-book smell of glue, paper, and must rises off the page from where it sits close to the spine. The dog beside me closes his eyes. His ears twitch every now and then. At night, the dogs on the street behind my room let loose around 2 or 3 a.m. I awake to their snarling low gruffs and high yips, thinking in the moments I pull out of sleep that it's something else I hear. I never remember what. My mind skips to half-sleep dreams, seeking to make connections in all I've taken in. I awake, restless and searching.

POSTCARD FROM ROLLOVER PASS

STEPHANIE DICKINSON

TEXAS CITY. I have carried my remembrances to this day-job cubicle where the rumble of the night maid's vacuum serenades my ears; I've lugged with me the dredged canals east of Galveston that run barges to the Gulf. Corralled into a clerical job, I still want the high of a Quaalude with its wicked name like a journey into a glacier or through a web, that split-second on the ledge; I want the buzz saw of mosquitoes, the smother of green from the live oaks and the afternoon's lull; I want the vision of the amberjack and sailtop catfish. In the here and now I force my fingers through their paces as the long ago boyfriend stops the Mercury Marquise at the pass. Reddish skin that bronzes in the sun, full lips, black hair, blacker eyes. All the older women winking, shaking their heads, "He's a beautiful man. Pity the girl." For a quick swim I float out into the barely moving backwater, a far-off radio playing the soft spoilage of Janis Joplin's voice. "Summertime" the shrimp grass warbles in its raw scent of weed sex. Then "Gimme a Pigfoot" wafts over the sand—Bessie Smith belting out the blue notes. Although I sense the undercurrent's roughness, I drift, sleepily. Then the flow grows forceful, dragging me into the channel—the thrust of an angry chute like the tongue baths at Bessie Smith's buffet flat. I still don't understand. I try to side-stroke toward the embankment, which barnacles cake—manes of dripping blue-black algae and shells sharpened into tin-can lids. I am caught by the strong water. Moss slimed my belly when I paddled, as if the undertow knew I was a weak swimmer, knew the snags were tugging me under, sucking my toes. I hailed from the Bible belt, the gunny sack shed girl, the widow's daughter who wasn't taught anything but to love God, and there I was calling on Him, all the while high and in lust with my dark-eyed lover, two years out of prison, a Dillinger-wanna-be. I couldn't beat back the current, brazen as dusky hogs in a wallow. Soon I would enter the Gulf and be hurled out to sea, when a Mexican boy, a stranger, dove in with a flash of skin and cutoffs, swimming toward me, and then my Dillinger, still wearing his metallic sunglasses, jack-knived into the water. They towed me to the embankment, where country folk, fishing, lowered their arms. Before I could thank him the boy ran off, vanishing. In the life since I've never stopped thinking how I owe him everything. The afternoon resumed its smell of cut bait and fresh death. Without these near misses who would I be? How else could I stand this gulag of wage slavery? I bartered my youth away yet I still want the sun and an iridescent oarfish all fifteen feet of deep sea ermine. Without those afternoons where you escape with your stupid life, I'd be an empty holler. My younger self and Dillinger pulled ourselves together and drove deeper into Texas, almost to its edge, where a smear of breeze would nudge us over the state line. What would any of us be without the sweet regret, that balloon of it, corded to us like a Portuguese Man-of-War?

AFLOAT

MARGOT KAHN

MY SON HAD been caring for two plastic penguins in a mixing bowl filled with water for six months, and I wanted my mixing bowl back. Finally, five weeks ago, the opportunity presented itself when he came home from preschool holding a paper cutout of a bowl. Inside the bowl, an orange handprint made the shape of a fish. He had drawn on a mouth and gills with a marker, and adhered two googly eyes with dollops of glue. "Look at my fish!" he said to me, beaming with pride. "I made it in the library!"

"I love it," I said. "How would you like to get a real fish as a pet?"

"Sure!" he said, eagerly, perhaps not completely comprehending what this meant.

I had been thinking about a pet for some time, since last year when we were reading Eric Carle's *A House for Hermit Crab* over and over again. But hermit crabs, a friend had warned me, lose their luster in a hurry, being nocturnal and all. Now, with my son four-and-a-half years old and having sustained an interest in sea creatures for more than a year, it seemed like a better time. A pet would be good for us, I thought. It would keep us company and demand some responsibility.

With several hours of afternoon still ahead of us, we drove to the pet store. Trotting up and down the aisles we chose a hydroponic tank that would grow real plants on the top, three freshwater snails, and an iridescent blue split-tail Betta fish.

"What will you call him?" I asked my son standing in the check-out line.

"Sweet Fish," he answered without hesitation, holding the plastic container aloft and gazing with great affection at this delicate, frightened thing.

And, admittedly to my surprise, my son happily fed Sweet Fish every day, dropping the tiny pellets into his tank, watching him swim, wondering why he went up or down, this way or that.

•••

Yesterday afternoon, I walked to the garden to pick some lettuce for dinner. And instead of listening to the world, to the birds chattering and the leaves shifting in a light breeze, I plugged myself into my phone and listened to Krista Tippet interview Mary Oliver.

"Lucretius presents this marvelous and important idea," Mary said sometime in the middle of the interview, "that what we are made of will make something else, which to me is very important. There is no nothingness with these little atoms that run around, too little for us to see, but put together they make something. And that to me is a miracle. Where it came from I don't know, but it's a miracle. And I think it's enough to keep a person afloat."

Whatever Mary said after that was lost on me. My mind wandered back to last week when Sweetie died. After a day of looking sickly, he had sunk to the bottom of the tank, dark and ragged, and the snails had started in on his feathery fins. By the time my son returned home from preschool there wasn't much of Sweetie left. If you looked closely, you could see part of his head poking out from beneath one of the Black Mystery snails.

"Where's Sweet Fish?" he asked me, peering into the tank.

"Bunny," I said, "I'm afraid Sweet Fish is dead."

"But where is he?"

"I'm afraid the snails have eaten him."

"Well," he said, matter-of-factly, "maybe we shouldn't have snails in the tank."

"Well," I replied, "it's just like the food web picture in your *Encyclopedia of Seas and Oceans*. Do you remember? How the dead fish breaks down into nutrients and becomes food for the other animals, like plankton? And the herring eat the plankton, and the tuna eat the herring, and the orca whale eats the tuna?" This was the only page of the *Encyclopedia of Seas and Oceans* he ever wanted to read, and we had read it now at least a hundred times. He thought a moment, nodded, and scampered off to find something to play with.

●●●

Last night, we took the lettuce I had picked and a mismatched six-pack from the fridge to our friends' house for dinner. The children and the dog played in the yard with a pool of water and some sticks and boats. We grilled pizza and sliced watermelon and listened to a woodpecker hammering away in a nearby tree. My friend, a practical, no-nonsense wife, mother, and engineer, said fish bowls are made for killing fish. She didn't mean it in an environmentalist sense, like she was going to boycott Petco for animal cruelty, though she is a lover of animals and outdoors and the natural world. She said it as a matter of fact, to make me understand that this death was not unusual or out of the ordinary or even my fault. Neither was she casting stones. She, too, had bought her children fish bowls and fish, and the fish had died. One of her children had been sad and the other hadn't noticed until two months later. "Where's my fishbowl?" her younger daughter, Wren, said, suddenly unable to find it in her room.

She told me, by way of commiserating, about the crow that was mortally wounded in the parking lot last week at her work. She pleaded with her team, for someone to go and put the bird out of its misery, and no one would. So she went herself and ran over the bird with her car. Birds are one of her great loves. Whenever I am with her she teaches me something— how to tell the difference between a raptor and a turkey vulture, how the hummingbird flies when it is looking for a mate. Her daughter, Wren, and my son were born four days apart.

After she killed the crow, she went into work and made some difficult decisions for her team. Then she took Wren to the doctor and held her while a blood vessel in her nose was cauterized to staunch the bleeding episodes that were waking her every night.

As we talked in the kitchen, the children were laughing, lounging in chairs holding triangles of pizza, putting their feet in the warm fur of the dog.

●●●

"You are keeping the humans in your house alive," said another friend after I told her about the fish. "That is enough."

"You are enough," said a friend who teaches yoga, repeating one of the tantra mantras she has passed on to us.

"It's the circle of life," said my husband. "Right?"

Yes.

So why had it shaken me so, the death of this fish that I knew would die at some point? I had deliberately declined buying the $20 water testing strips sold at the pet store for checking the pH and nitrogen levels of the water. "I don't care about the fish that much," I'd said to the fish specialist, and then felt rotten for saying it. I wasn't even sure if I meant it. I knew I would care if the fish died before the year was out, before it had had time to live a full life, before we had loved it and learned to care for another living being.

Oh, Mary. Mary. Lucretius. Lucretius. What we are made of will make something else. There is no nothingness with these little atoms that run around, too little for us to see. It is enough to keep a person afloat.

●●●

Five days ago, my son looked into the tank and said, "We don't have a pet."

"We have three snails!" I said.

"But we don't have a fish."

"No," I relented. "We don't. Would you like to get another fish and try again?"

"Yes," he said. "I would like to try again."

"Alright," I said. "Alright. We will try again."

FLYING CAVE BEAR

SARAH SHEESLEY

GIRAFFE SALIVA IS among the best antibacterial substances in the world. It protects their tongues from infection after eating thorny tree branches and the knife-edges of leaves. I want my arms and neck to be licked by giraffes. I want to visit a giraffe at the end of the day to clean my hands and seal my paper cuts. I want its neck to lean against mine, and feel the blood coursing through its thick vertical veins. It comforts me to know that giraffes exist—that they are both gentle and ferocious, both graceful and awkward, and that right now they are blinking their furry long-lashed eyelids over their dark farsighted eyes. The giraffe slips a baby from her uterus while ambling through the bush. The calf is covered in spots and slime, and already walking. The giraffe spreads its front legs wide, and bends down low to the water. When it drinks it is only drinking, slipping its long tongue into muddy water.

I didn't go to Kenya looking for giraffes, and I don't think of myself as an animal person. I took the trip because when I'm feeling lost and flush with imaginary wealth, I tend to travel. I wanted to be more alive than I felt at the time, and more alive than I feel in general. I wanted to see the Great Rift Valley, the birthplace of humankind. I went with friends and ate tons of food and drank Tusker and mango juice and gin and went to parties and big city clubs and shopping malls and bought souvenirs and rode around in safari vans and went to small villages and visited an elephant orphanage.

At the orphanage I slathered sunscreen on my pale December skin, suddenly exposed to equatorial light. We lined up and waited with a hundred other tourists to watch the elephants come down to the crowd for their daily feeding of special elephant formula from a baby bottle the size of a man's arm. A guide came out and taught about poaching and the human/wildlife land conflict, the shrinking habitat, hungry farmers, and the babies who wander and cry and starve without their massive mamas. The herd tromped down to be fed and paraded themselves around for the audience—flapping ears and kicking up dust, trunks crawling over each other's backs and wrapping around the arms of their keepers. A baby elephant cannot be left alone. Ever. They sleep with their keeper, wake together, walk together. Without company the elephant falls into despair and fails to thrive. I decide to become an elephant keeper. I have no job to return to, no life plan. There is nothing else for me. I will dedicate my life to the well-being of elephants. I will sleep on a cot in a stable, grow strong shoveling dung, bottle feed and pat the bellies of elephants as I grow into an old, wrinkled woman in the company of profound enormity. I reach out to touch the smallest one as he trots by. My touch is like everyone else's—quick and light and awestruck on the cement-textured skin.

Of course I did not become an elephant keeper. The people I've shared that sentiment with tend to think I want intimacy, or companionship, or perhaps a baby. No. I want a singleness of purpose. I want boundaries that eliminate all other obligation, and all other options. Of course the real elephant keepers probably don't feel this. I bet they feel burdened by their needy charge. I bet they want a few days off to visit family in some distant village. I bet their girlfriends wish they didn't smell like elephant. I bet they secretly hate the tourists. I just want to focus on survival. Keep myself alive. Keep the elephant alive. Eat. Run. Sleep.

At the time I was dating someone who constantly explained to me that he was in "survival mode." Not the survival mode of an eagle when it spots its prey from the sky or shares its kill with the young, or a mouse finding cover in winter, or a squirrel gathering nuts. His survival mode was more like a fish in a bucket.

On the southern coast of Kenya, the trade winds blow warm and damp and constant through the house—the same winds that drove merchants up and down the coast since forever. Alone with the wind on a dark balcony, I want to lift my damp sundress to the moon and the hands of the air. An unexpected peep show for the Masai night watchman standing silently in the thick shadows with his spear, guarding us from who knows what. Making money for his family somewhere or his own life in the village. *I wish I would get captured by Somali pirates*, I think. Of course I don't wish that. But then I could really get away from it all. I wish I were on Zanzibar. I wish I were alone. I wait for an epiphany. It doesn't come. I want to be a Somali pirate.

I don't want to be a Somali pirate. I want comfort and security. I want my home to be a cozy cliffside nest a mile high. I want to sleep hard through the winter. I want to carry my children in my mouth.

Posters on the walls of the rental house show the fish of the Seychelles labeled in French. I consider barracudas. Long cylindrical silvery bodies like thick shiny arrows with sharp teeth. I've been told they can bite your arm off under water and tear it to shreds. The smell of blood will attract sharks, and you will end up a mess of flesh in a salty, inky cloud of blood.

I don't know if this is true. We ate a barracuda for dinner. It was a fish curry with vegetables and rice—delicate and delicious.

If you met me, you would see an average middle class white American woman in reasonably good shape, reasonably poised, relatively well dressed with dark blonde hair. No piercings or tattoos. I treat people well. I shop organic. Online quizzes categorize me as "urbane." A teacher once commented that, "It must be hard to rebel when you look like that." I think she meant that I look *good*. I envy the hippo. I wish there were threatening signs about me, posted in the hotel lobby. "CAUTION. Girl may bite you to death." But I am well trained in nonviolent conflict resolution. I know not to spend my days wallowing in the cool mud. Not to let birds sit on my head. Not to ignore parasitic insects.

Someone recently asked me what animal (real or mythical) I would be if I could choose anything, and without much thought I said a flying bear. He asked me what kind of bear, and I said maybe a grizzly, and he said, "Maybe a cave bear? They're even bigger than grizzlies (though extinct)."

"Yes, a flying cave bear," I confirmed. I want to fly. I want to be huge and have thick fur and hibernate and eat blackberries or the flesh of a newborn elk. I wish my tongue were eighteen inches long. I wish I could hear moth wings beat a block away. I wish I could smell you and know your history better than you know it yourself. I wish I could run easily at 80 mph. I wish that traveling could fix this.

LETTER FROM THE PSYCHIATRIC WARD

JESSI TERSON

NOW I KNOW what you're thinking. Why the hell am I writing with a completely blunted pencil? Can't I see the words are smudging? Leaving behind nothing but a gray, dribbling river? Clearly, the rumors are true. I've completely lost my mind.

But, no. It's just that at some point in the history of mental health care, a patient was forced to be resourceful. And apparently wielding an HB graphite #2 is a perfectly good way to gouge out someone's eye. Still, the nurses are smarter. You should see the way they strut around, the tips of their big brains protruding like giant hard-ons against their brows. So of course, in a sudden burst of inspiration, they came up with a solution. No more sharpened pencils. Ever! In fact, I'm pretty sure this particular tip began eroding in the early nineties. Really, it's a shame that I'm not actually crazy. The letters bleed into each other so nicely, forming a perfectly dirty lake to drown my face in. If only I thought it was real.

Sadly, almost everything real is forbidden. Even personalized pillowcases. It's true. Read the ICU contraband list. No musical instruments. No provocative material (luckily none of the nurses seem to have read *Lolita*, as it slipped past their radar and now rests discreetly on my lap—dangerously close to my crotch, mind you!). No pens. Though really, I suppose I should get down on my knees and shout Hallelujah anyway. At least these places no longer perform lobotomies. The contraband list from the 1960s probably included a vibrant right hemisphere of the brain.

Though God knows, if I'm going to survive here, I need one. Don't be fooled by that one novel I know you were forced to read in high school. Ken Kesey was out of his mind. Believe me, this place could never be a source of inspiration. Not the black bars hung like crucifixes on the window panes. Not the shit-stains splattered on the chairs. And certainly not the other patients. Because let me tell you a secret. The average crazy person is boring. Perhaps they're too pumped full of drugs. Most of them just sit quietly in their chairs. Occasionally a person will randomly stand up, as if some part of his id recalled the long lost game of musical chairs. For a few minutes he'll look to the person at his right. If he's particularly animated, a brown splotch might appear on the bottom of his white pajamas pants, like an inkblot on a Rorschach card. Oh yes. You should see it. That one there—it looks exactly like a moth. (God, can't they realize how normal I am? Seeing exactly what I'm supposed to see? Let the next person shit, and I promise, I'll see the card with the bat.)

Eventually the poor patient sits down and presses his psychological imprint back into the chair. Once again, there is nothing for me to notice. Just another patient staring into space, waiting for the music in his head to start up again.

God. Please forgive this particularly bleary streak of graphite. My pencil continues to flatten. Which is fitting. Because really, it sort of feels like a blunted pencil is slowly picking away at my heart. A kind of Chinese water torture. After the first few watery gray paragraphs, it's pretty easy to fall apart. Not that I need to blame a synapse misfiring. Poopstains would make anyone depressed. Welcome to the human condition. Everyone poops. I guess just not everyone uses a toilet.

I just asked one nurse if she'd let me have my novel to work on, as they're holding most of my possessions behind the front desk. But she only gave me a look that said, "Get lost." Now with just one corridor to walk back and forth down, that's pretty impossible. Though I suppose I could do myself a favor and get lost in my own head. They only need to up my dosage of lithium. My brain will be flaccid in no time.

Oh, and it's freezing up here. Apparently the furnace broke. The air is so cold that I can see my own breath. In the effort to combat hypothermia, they've been passing out extra blankets. Now one of the schizophrenics is too swaddled to properly flail her arms. She frantically bats at the fabric—a rabid butterfly half-caught in her cocoon. I myself am wearing every sweater I brought here. I must look ineffectual. Like a soft, fat blob. Not like the man who walks past me: his blanket strapped to his chest like a bomb.

The nurses begin to take away our pencils. Something about it being "rest time." I politely asked if I could keep writing this letter, as I obviously wouldn't be disturbing anyone. But the answer was an unequivocal NO. Maybe it's the freezing temperature or the rolling mounds of patients slumped over in their chairs, but suddenly, I want to flail my arms too. I want to scream, "Don't you know that words are anchors!? Solid things that root us to the world, when the world is slipping by!?" But I forget. I'm supposed to get lost. . . .

Well, my pencil was confiscated for an hour. The bedrooms are even colder than the commons room, so my roommate and I buried ourselves under our blankets. She's only a kid. Nineteen at the most. Her eyes are so glassy, it's like someone dug out her eyeballs and replaced them with marbles. Every time she smiles, I worry the mechanism holding her face together will bust. Her head will fall off and roll down the hallway. The schizophrenic will give it a kick; and before I know it, the entire psych ward will have started a a game of soccer. By tomorrow, decapitated heads will also be on the ICU contraband list.

I just made the mistake of glancing around the commons room. The other patients have this uncanny ability to do nothing but stare into space. What the hell are they seeing? And if I have to be here, why the hell can't I hallucinate too? As if sensing this, some of the patients keep telling me that I look like a normal person. I'm not sure if I'm suppose to apologize or not. Does wanting to stab the center of the world with a blunted pencil make me crazy? I don't know. That question never showed up on the psychiatric assessment.

I'm sorry this letter goes on and on. If they'd just let me work on my novel, I'd stop harassing you. But they still won't give me my manuscript. I guess it's too dangerous. That's 110 pages of potential paper airplanes. I could start a military raid! Bomb the nurses' station!

A particularly snide nurse just gave me a new blank piece of paper and said, "Here. In case you get any brilliant ideas." I'd like to fold it into an origami crane and tell her to go fly herself to hell. But that would be one less page to write on. When my father hugged me goodbye last night, he urged me to make the best of the situation. "Just remember," he said. "Everything is material. Write about this place."

On another note, I smell bad. They won't give me any deodorant. And it's too cold to shower. If you end up coming to visit me, I suggest you bring nose plugs. And maybe, just to be safe, a diaper. This place is so boring, I'm thinking of shitting my pants too. Everything for material, right?

If my thoughts seem scattered, forgive me. Really, they're only interrupted. A lot goes on here. The nurses keep taking my vitals. Apparently my pulse is weak. Lucky me. Maybe I won't have to kill myself after all.

But in the meantime, I do my best to occupy the time. For a few minutes I watch the young man beside me. He sits perfectly still—with eyes closed and a gentle smile on his lips. As if his shit-stained chair was some thousand-petaled lotus. And because God knows I have nothing better to do, I decide to close my eyes too. I picture a giant vacuum sucking up my thoughts. And when that doesn't work, I try to imagine my brain as something already empty. A hollow seashell. But you've held one to your ear. They say you can still hear the ocean. Even if you're sane.

A young woman I hadn't noticed just sat down next to me. Her pajama sleeves are rolled up, exposing the scars on her arms. Christ! She is not the average cutter. Five red stars, the lines unbelievably symmetrical, blaze across her flesh. Only the last star is incomplete. Its second point juts out, suddenly, as if on a random impulse, straight to her wrist (where, apparently, she found the victory vein). But maybe she had planned it that way from the beginning. Perhaps she was only trying to create something beautiful. One last time. I'd like to tell her they're pretty. But that can't be the right thing to say. Somewhere in the world, someone would disapprove.

As if on cue, three nurses enter the room. They stand there, the grays of their scrubs touching, so together, they form one giant cloud. Look at them! So eager to rain on our parade! Unfortunately, no one is misbehaving. Unless you count the audacity of this young woman forcing me to witness her suffering. Well, hang some goddamn art on the walls you cumulus smears, and I guarantee, I'll look at something else.

In an extraordinary demonstration of interpersonal skills, the young woman asks me what my name is. Her voice is almost unbearably soft. Like her words are a gauze that just might rip apart in her mouth. For a few minutes we talk. Not about anything particularly important. We don't discuss our diagnoses. Or why we're here. Though I suppose in her case, it's spelled out in red lights. We don't mention our day jobs or our age. Instead she confides that she's on her period. She's not allowed to wear tampons. (Another item on the ICU contraband list. God forbid some girl has a neck the size of an asparagus stick and tries to hang herself with the little white string.) So, for the first time since she was thirteen, she's wearing a pad. She tells me how when she goes to pee, she can see the blood gush out in thick, clotted ribbons. "So much blood," she says and looks at her wrist. "What a joke."

And then she takes my pencil and examines the tip. She presses her thumb onto the graphite, but it barely makes an indentation. I have no idea what to say, so I just say something stupid. "The pen is mightier than the sword."

For a second she looks at me to see if I'm being serious. And then, abruptly, she bursts out laughing. And maybe it's only because I'm so grateful for the sound of something that almost seems like joy, but I feel the light start in the center of my chest—in the gap between my lungs. For a moment my body goes numb, in anticipation of what's about to happen. I close my eyes and take one last look at what's still the darkness in my body. Then, like the sun rising over the empty surface of a lake, the light spills over, shining through me and out to everything else in the room. I don't know whether to call it happiness. I never have. It never seemed like happiness should physically hurt. Like standing in the center of a prism— the light flashing in a hundred different directions.

And just like that, the light goes out. A man I know from intensive outpatient therapy just walked into the room. His name is Donald. He's an old man. Or at least he looks like one. He moves in short little jerks, as if his insides were precariously stacked with dishes. Normally, when he sits down, he folds his hands in his lap and stares at his shoes. (Though now the laces have been confiscated. Another item obviously on the contraband list.) I'd like to give him the string of a balloon to clasp. *Not* because I want to watch the poor man hang himself. It just pains me to see him so lost. Without a string connecting him to a place where maybe, just maybe, suffering no longer exists.

When I saw him, I ran into his arms. And even though we had only spoken a handful of times in the outside world, he gladly hugged me back. Funny how love exists, no matter where you go. I suppose, if we're lucky, we bring it with us. . . .

Another interlude. I just found out I'm getting released tonight. It's strange, but I should be happier. It's just that now Donald and the woman covered in red stars resent me. They don't mean to. But I can see the distance in their eyes. Not that I can blame them. I mean, when does a patient ever get released after only one night? Without knowing anything, I know it was my father who helped me. I saw the look in his eyes when he hugged me goodbye.

I was ten years old when I first learned about hell (*not,* of course, from my liberal Jewish father). And I remember thinking that such a place was impossible. God would want everyone to go to heaven, because even *I* wanted everyone to go heaven. Even if they didn't belong there. Now maybe tomorrow my family will go out to dinner. I'll sit in the booth and wear my bloody wrists like bangles, waiting for a song to start so I can stand up and look forlornly to the person at my right. And my father will look at his shoelaces, wishing it was possible to lace everything up. Even the hole in the center of my chest. Even the world, with all of its broken pieces. And broken people who don't belong.

Well, I am now back at my parents' home. Luckily for you, at least the very last part of this monstrosity of a letter will be neatly penned in black ink. God, isn't it lovely? The way each letter keeps to itself? The ink its own kind of straight jacket?

As tempted as I am to keep writing you another twenty pages, I suppose I should try to prove that I'm sane. Which I'm pretty sure equates to something like shutting up. But really, thank you for letting me ramble.

And this is the part of the letter where I go to sign my name. I consider including a P.S. where I apologize for what I did. Or I could try to make my excuses. But you don't give a damn about stars. I know that. And besides, I didn't have the foresight to make one. My decision was sloppy. A splotch of red that doesn't look like anything. Not a moth. Not a bat.

But darling, these are only words. It doesn't take a pencil to make them smudge and disappear. And I don't expect you to understand what I would say, if I knew how to say it. But please, put a seashell to your ear and listen to that sound. Though they say it's not really the ocean. My anchors are there. Where nothing is real. And of course, nothing forbidden. Do you hear them? Please. Tell me you hear them.

THIS IS NOT AN EKPHRASTIC POEM

CHARLES HOOD

BUT NEVER MIND that now, and instead, in appreciation of Rousseau, *Scouts Attacked by a Tiger*, I just need to say that from here on out, obviously all tigers should be shaped like accordions, and what about the dead scout, floral in a yellow muumuu and floating on blades of grass as tall as Rousseau on Sunday horseback, the dead scout dreaming of violins

even as *Le Douanier* paints and paints, singing. Stage left, the moon-sun hides the daylight inside the butter. Scout 2 rides his horse like dirty laundry, laundry that rides a horse that doubles as a stingray. Even the gilded frame writhes, bouquet of fingertips. Still, never mind the frame, it's that tiger—we must do something. Shouldn't we do something? I would sell my children

to paint like this—no, that's not true. I would sell my children and some of yours too to be the kind of man who could sell his children for smears of paint. Welcome to the new France: even the iron scrollwork applauds. White pullets in the coop, dirigible-bodied children swollen under hot air balloons, sashes with medals: good morning, 1904. It makes me

want to paint my lawn again and again until (like Rousseau's) it can comb its hair with daylight. No, I want to break into the frame and steal the air trapped inside wads of paint, Rousseau's breath pressed into the pigment like black ants in red amber. Lick the painting and you lick his hands, his face. Drill a hole in the frame and blow out the yolk,

save the meaning in a perfect oology of genius. Rousseau does not need us; the scouts though do, they are Hindu or probably Muslim, and there is nobody on hand to wash their bodies, say the right prayers, lay them out in honor. Every painting implies a *what's next*, and we need to hurry up, the tiger is slaughtering these poor men.

Maybe we could tranquilize the beast, relocate it to some meadow of fruit trees and masochistic deer, deer that maybe were all war criminals once, so they deserve to die. Maybe the tiger is a Buddhist, wants to be vegetarian, just give it a chance. Maybe it will get bored, fall asleep. Maybe tigers are afraid of masks. Put this on. What would Picasso do?

Maybe I will hide in a toilet stall in the men's room: after closing, when the guard kills the lights, I will still be there waiting, just me and Picasso and a few hired guns, all waiting to lock and load and climb inside the picture and when I give the signal, ready to rush to help repopulate the sad and desperate world

of *Scouts Attacked by a Tiger*, oil on canvas, Barnes Foundation, Philadelphia, USA.

REVIEWS

EDITED BY ALYSE BENSEL

REVIEWS

Whatever Became of Fun-to-Read?

Charles Harper Webb

THE OTHER ODYSSEY, RICHARD GARCIA; DREAM HORSE PRESS, 2014
ISBN: 978-1935716280; $17.65; 110 PP.

SUGAR RUN ROAD, ED OCHESTER; AUTUMN HOUSE PRESS, 2015
ISBN: 978-1938769016; $17.95; 80 PP.

SLICE OF MOON, KIM DOWER; RED HEN PRESS, 2013
ISBN: 978-1597099714; $18.95; 102 PP.

PUT THIS ON, PLEASE: NEW & SELECTED POEMS, WILLIAM TROWBRIDGE;
RED HEN PRESS, 2014
ISBN: 978-1597099660; $19.95; 203 PP.

READING REVIEWS OF poetry, I sometimes feel like an undergrad hearing Professor Dingle-blort explicate Ezra Pound's *Selected Water Bills*. Like the books they review, the reviews I'm speaking of aren't fun to read. Amid talk of Sapphics, dystichs, and arcane prosodies, of disjunctivity and discontinuity, unproblematization, under-theorization, hegemonies of oppression, meanings that wiggle/shift/evaporate, there's not much room for fun.

In the pack of literary values, fun seems to be analogous to the Inuits' "least respected dog." And yet, if more poems were more fun, more people, by definition, would like poems.

As well as being fun to read, the collections discussed below contain as much intelligence, subtlety of perception, emotional resonance, political awareness, and insight into the human condition as any books of poems being written today. I say this with confidence, because the poems aren't camouflaged in fashionable obscurity.

As American poetry's profile sinks below sea level, I'm glad to celebrate four books that, if better known, could push that profile up.

•••

Richard Garcia's poetry is poignant, wildly imaginative, and sometimes hilarious. I like the title of his book *The Other Odyssey* so much that I'm now writing *The Other Iliad*. Garcia's poems move with the logic of dreams. Always fresh and surprising, they are never gratuitously weird. Their imagery springs not from a conscious wish to confound readers with strangeness, but from the deep unconscious, which draws inspiration and power from the physical world. Garcia's poems are often surreal, but always grounded in human reality.

A series of three poems about unusual museums introduce us to The Museum of Songs You Can't Remember, The Museum of Clothespins (a small section in The Museum of Fasteners), The Museum of Dog Barks (including the wheeze of the dingo, which doesn't bark), The Museum of Souls (which are, of course, invisible), and naturally, The Museum of Lost Single Socks. (Did you know that Genghis Khan means *One Sock*, or *He of the Missing Sock*? You do now.)

These "museums," though funny, aren't jokes. They express, in a strangely moving way, the human need to admire and preserve the objects of our transient world. "Offbeat Museums" ends with an image of unearthly earthly beauty: "In the Cafeteria of the Museum of Dawn / be sure to try the slice of yellow light / served on a deep blue platter."

Garcia's poems are often powered by longing. Ulysses ends his days

> not thinking of Calypso,
>
> turning his mind to the way everything,
>
> the sand, the walls of the cave, the vault
>
> of the stars, would rise and fall, waver
>
> like the sea, like her breathing . . .

His poem "Louise" speaks of a woman who may be a waitress in a Waffle House, whose name may not even be Louise, but for whom the speaker, who may or may not be a busboy or dish-washer, pines.

> Louise, always in a hurry
>
> . . . The Waffle
>
> House Fun Facts could
>
> be our Waffle House
>
> Fun Facts . . . Waffle House Boogie
>
> could be our song.

The Other Odyssey takes the reader on an odyssey of the mind. The adventures we encounter are sometimes dangerous, sometimes unsettling, often moving and beautiful, but always fun.

• • •

Ed Ochester is a different sort of poet, but just as much fun: a poet of plain speech, acerbic wit, and deep compassion for and insight into humankind. *Sugar Run Road* is short on post-post-modern devices meant to disorient the reader, and long on concrete details from the lived world. Many of the poems are narratives: the story of how Boston cops responded to the young Ochester's teaching *The Catcher in the Rye*; the story of how Ochester happened upon Edward Field's *Stand Up Friend With Me*, and how that book "metaphorically and just / possibly literally / saved my life."

I say *Ochester* because the poems insist upon their own facticity. Not for Ed O is that staple of creative writing workshop, the "speaker." Ochester speaks for himself—clearly, entertainingly, and well.

His poems embody the aesthetic, which he articulates in "Riding Westward." "I argue for the heart . . . [not] 'challenging' poetry which / often means I think 'obscure,' / the speaker refusing to tell / what he knows."

"I like complexity," Ochester says, "not confusion / plain surface texture / free of mere complicatedness . . ."

Ochester also likes humor—likes it a lot, as evidenced by "Conan the Librarian," who discovers that "he adores Frank O'Hara, loves to quote: / 'dod painting's nod so blue' and / 'Lana Durner ve luff you, ged up!'"

Like William Carlos Williams, Ochester celebrates the concrete *things* of this world: crows, friends, sunflowers, the city of Pittsburgh, the Penguins, bad but enthusiastic singing, his granddaughter, the word *penis*, and his wife Britt. His barbed satiric vision deflates, among other things, government officials, the pretensions of universities, and the concept of "the decorum of a Marriott."

For a funny and disturbing commentary on Roman history and contemporary poetry, I recommend "what you should know about the emperor nero."

For a great read, cover to cover, I recommend *Sugar Run Road*.

• • •

Kim Dower's latest collection, *Slice of Moon,* is witty, sexy, irreverent, touching, and disarmingly candid. Attuned to life's quirky and endearing strangeness, her poems are, you guessed it, *fun*.

In "Bottled Water," the poet mocks and celebrates the verbal magic that changes regular old water into "Glitter Geyser" and "Deer Park," not to mention "Real Water" and "Smart Water." "If I drink Smart Water," Dower asks,

> will I raise my IQ but be less authentic?
> If I choose Real Water will I no longer
> deny the truth, but will I attract confused
> needy people who'll take advantage
> of my realness by dumping their problems
> on me, and I will be too stupid to help them . . .

It's a fine send-up; yet, like good poetry, the water-names call up images so strong our brains accept them as (well, almost) true. Having consumed, just to be safe, bottles of both Real Water *and* Smart Water, our heroine can walk the streets ". . . with a new swagger / knowing the world is mine."

Not all of Dower's poems are as funny as "Bottled Water." Yet even those composed in minor keys—poems such as "I Lost My Mother at Bloomingdale's" and "Ninth Grade Boyfriend"—return us to our own frail, mortal skins, re-dedicated and renewed.

In "Boob Job," the poem's heroine, while trying on clothes at Loehmann's, helps another woman zip up a dress too small for her newly-enhanced breasts.

"Do you want to feel them," she [the other woman] asks . . ." "It's not sexual," she insists. Still, it's a steamy scene, both women trading feels as the poem considers the mysteries of "boob men" versus "ass men," and what exactly an "ass job" would be.

The women, Dower says, forget "how it felt when we were twelve / or thirteen, one morning when they first appeared / sore, swollen, exciting, new, when they had the power / to turn us into women we no longer knew." The women in the poem forget, but the poet does not.

Neither, because of her, do we.

• • •

William Trowbridge—widely admired for his wit—is a master at dealing with American boyhood, popular culture, and mid-twentieth century history, both public and personal.

He is, as Thomas Lux states, a poet of plain speech and a master of metaphor, the power of which can lift his plain speech into the empyrean.

Put This On Please: New & Selected Poems gives readers a taste of Trowbridge from 1989 to the present. Its 200-plus pages are packed with riches from the first poem, "Stark Weather"—as spare and stark as the Great Plains where Charles Starkweather did his dirty deeds—to "Unofficial Missouri Poem," which takes a lovingly satirical look at the "Show Me" State, of which Trowbridge is Poet Laureate. With apologies to *Kong* and *Fool*, who preside over whole sections of this book, I'll focus on two poems.

The first, "Mr. Fix It," portrays Dad as Schlemiel: Dad—for whom "screws talked back, nails went / rubbery, saws turned piraña"—cursing his tools and his fate as nothing he does around the house goes right. Yet the poem becomes an off-beat elegy. The hapless dad, a veteran of World War II with two Bronze Stars, is a hero brought low by the quotidian. When the canister of "Gro-Brite" he buys, hoping for a golf-course-quality lawn, blows up in his face, "the metal lid grazing an ear," I laugh. But I also hope that, faced with my own daily travails, I'll find the guts to "soldier on" half so nobly.

Another favorite poem in this book of favorites is "Coach Said." What Coach actually said—"No water during football practice"—turns out to be stupid, ill-informed, and close to criminal. But what he meant—what he was trying to do—was to give his team the key to victory that had always eluded him. Instead of thinking, *that hard-nosed dolt,* I end the poem thinking, *That poor, frustrated, groping-in-the-dark son-of-a-bitch could be me.*

This is the triumph of Trowbridge's poems. The characters that inhabit them are all unique—all absolutely, particularly themselves. Yet, as they struggle, again and again, to stand up after life's pratfalls, they are us, too. They are everyone.

THE USES OF THE BODY

POETRY BY DEBORAH LANDAU

COPPER CANYON PRESS, 2015; ISBN: 978-1556594816; $16.00; 65 PP.
REVIEWED BY BETH SUTTON-RAMSPECK AND DOUG RAMSPECK

FOR CENTURIES OUR species has focused on the mind/body split. Plato believed that the two were connected only until the body was shed like a snakeskin, and the soul remained to consort with the eternal truths.

In Deborah Landau's third book of poems, the poet explores a different kind of mind/body separation. The speakers appear divided from their own lives, occasionally dispassionate, other times bemused or critical or horrified. The very title expresses the split: "the body"—not "my body"—is examined in a series of linked narratives: a wedding, sex, illness, death, births. The distance from which these events are viewed creates a cascade of beautiful ironies and humorous horrors. In the "thick last week" of pregnancy, for example, a speaker observes in a detached, unsentimental, but still emotionally laden language,

> The teleprompter reads liberty reads hosiery
>
> Reads zany, loose, glucose, says get ready
> To plonk one out.
>
> A birth, a hurdle to vault, and then the toes
> The scum, the potty and bumpers of it.

In *The Uses of the Body,* Landau approaches our ancient preoccupations in a way that feels original, startling, and, in places, breathtaking.

FIFTEEN DOGS

FICTION BY ANDRÉ ALEXIS

COACH HOUSE BOOKS, 2015; ISBN: 978-1552453056; $17.95; 160 PP.
REVIEWED BY STEPHANIE BARBÉ HAMMER

We will have no masters, said Atticus. Dogs without masters are the only true dogs.

THE PHILOSOPHICAL DOG has been with us as a literary trope since at least Plato with excursions through Aesop, Rabelais, Kafka, and yes, even Richard Adams. But novelist André Alexis is undaunted by this intimidating history; *Fifteen Dogs* brilliantly and at times horrifically attacks the classical metaphor straight on by having Hermes and Apollo make a bet about humans and language in a bar near a veterinary clinic. What follows meshes *Animal Farm*, *Lord of the Flies*, and *the Decameron*, with more than a passing nod to Kafka's long short story *Investigations of a Dog* and some indirect digs at *Lassie*. *Fifteen Dogs* shouldn't work, but does, because of its absolutely gorgeous language, and its determination to follow the power dynamics between talking dogs and humans to their logical, extreme conclusions. The result is a surreal yet completely understandable set of adventures that examine gang identity, sex, masculinity, difference, artistry, memory, and how language fails us, and how it doesn't.

> There was no clearly compelling reason to be optimistic about a dog that spent its time composing (and remembering) poems in a language unknown to all but a diminishing handful of dogs . . . And yet there was something. Prince's wit, his playfulness, was a curious element within him, a glittering depth.

Not for the faint hearted, this novel raises disturbing questions about human beings' relationship to other sentient creatures and to our sense of ourselves—still—as the center of creation. This is a unique, unforgettable piece of writing.

MULTIPLY/DIVIDE: ON THE AMERICAN REAL AND SURREAL
NONFICTION BY WENDY S. WALTERS

SARABANDE BOOKS, AUGUST 2015; ISBN: 978-1941411049; $15.95; 216 PP.
REVIEWED BY B.J. HOLLARS

UPON ARRIVING IN New Orleans in the aftermath of Hurricane Katrina, Wendy S. Walters soon finds herself searching for her outrage. Yet despite her efforts, Walters admits that she cannot home in on "a singular source of outrage on which to fixate—not poverty, racism, the failure of the federal government," or any other matter. It's her lack of outrage that clues Walters into her "profound sense of disconnection," forcing her to consider her expectations of America, as well as her place in it. "Lonely in America"—*Multiply/Divide*'s opening essay—continues by recounting Walters's personal journey to connect with her country and countrymen, ultimately leading her from the storm-ravaged South to the niceties of the North. But her visit to Portsmouth, New Hampshire reveals that these niceties hardly hold up beneath the surface. When a construction crew unearths the remains of several slaves, Walters is forced to begin her own personal excavation of what it means to be a descendant of slaves, a stranger in a familiar land. Her examination of loneliness manifests itself throughout the remainder of her genre-bending collection—from a fictional interview with an experimental playwright to the very real depiction of an innocent stroll with her child gone awry. While Walters often refers to her "lack of feeling" and feeling "unmoved," the problem is that readers, too, are forced to face that mostly muted feeling. How can we participate when we are not invited in? How can we share in the outrage when the outrage is not shared? Unquestionably, Walters risks alienating readers by leaving them alone and disconnected on the outside looking in—though, ultimately, that might just be her point.

GIVING UP

FICTION BY MIKE STEEVES

BOOKTHUG, 2015; ISBN: 978-1771660914; $20.00; 256 PP.
REVIEWED BY DANIEL PECCHENINO

NEAR THE END of Mike Steeves's monologic novel, Mary, one half of a couple in the midst of a prolonged slide into permanent resignation, thinks: "Life together is too complex." On one level, she's talking about her relationship with James, a basement tinkerer in love with the sound of his own voice, but also secretly sure that he's completely ruined his life (and Mary's) by devoting himself to a never-named and likely never-to-be-finished project. More importantly though, Mary is articulating an apprehension that has probably hung over each successive generation of bourgeois urbanites: that life now is bigger, faster, and more overwhelming than ever before, and that we missed out on an earlier, simpler golden age.

If Mary and James sound like whiners, don't worry, they're harder on themselves than any reader ever could be. That both are so simultaneously self-absorbed and witheringly self-deprecating makes *Giving Up* a fun read, but also one that thinks through important cultural problems: financial precarity, fertility anxiety, the intoxicating falseness of keeping up with both the social media Joneses and the "extraordinary men and women" who make their dreams come true after "toil[ing] away in obscurity for years and years."

Like Philip Roth's Alexander Portnoy and Salinger's Holden Caulfield in their respective books, James's and Mary's inner-thoughts drive *Giving Up* down hysterical backroad tangents and into sad little philosophical cul-de-sacs. Their voices are distinct, but share a similar acidic comic edge that makes it clear why they ended up together. While the lack of paragraph breaks might turn off readers who want permission to walk away every now and then, Steeves packs so many of the couples we all know into two characters and 200 pages that you just might finish *Giving Up* in one sitting.

LOOMING

POETRY BY JENNIFER FRANKLIN

ELIXIR PRESS, 2015; ISBN: 978-1932418545; $17.00; 88 PP.
REVIEWED BY ALYSE BENSEL

JENNIFER FRANKLIN'S DEBUT poetry collection *Looming* speaks to irrevocable loss, mourning, and struggle. Both the art and act of looming engulf these poems, which unfolds and repeats tragedy after tragedy. The opening poem, "Daughter," immediately strings together this tension: ". . . I am the unloved // Necessity. I am the quiet in a hall / When the music ceases. Someday, / I will surprise them with opacity." Then, the mother chimes in, crafting her own story amidst her daughter's narrative that has been stifled due to brain damage. In "All the Peloponnesian wildflowers will not bring you back," the mother tells her daughter, "It took me years to realize that nothing / Could save you. And no matter how much / I brought or bought you, I could not / Restore your lighthearted laugh." These repeated failures, as much *ars poetica* as speaking of her daughter, are bitterly acknowledged in the poem's final lines: "But the atrocious ability to create does not include / The power to heal what cannot be fixed." A mother in endless pursuit of her daughter, echoing and reshaping the myth of Demeter and Persephone, *Looming* persistently embraces the lyric tradition to relate an oftentimes unknowable suffering.

BY THE BOOK:
STORIES AND PICTURES
SHORT FICTION BY DIANE SCHOEMPERLEN

BIBLIOASIS, 2014; ISBN: 978-1927428818; $28.95; 224 PP.
REVIEWED BY PEDRO PONCE

THE TITLE OF Diane Schoemperlen's latest collection suggests what puts off many readers about conceptual writing: its emphasis on structure rather than motivated plot, language rather than character psychology. But Schoemperlen's approach is much less schematic, as she explains in her introduction: "The seven stories in this collection are based in various ways on old texts from the late nineteenth and early twentieth centuries. In the tradition of the *objet trouvé*, especially found in poetry, these stories take the form of a found narrative: an imagined, expanded, and embroidered rearrangement of the original material" (author's italics). The results are playful, provocative, revealing, and unsettling. In the title story, "By the Book or: Alessandro in the New World," Alessandro immigrates to the United States with the help of a guidebook inherited from his great-great-great-grandfather. Alessandro's narrative is interspersed with excerpts from Schoemperlen's source text, *Nuovissima Grammatica Accelerata* from 1900. The juxtaposition of tale and text humorously exposes the clash of immigrant aspirations with the prejudices of his adopted homeland. "History Becomes Authentic," her reassembly of Charles E. Little's *The Cyclopedia of Classified Dates With An Exhaustive Index*, collapses human history into a cyclical narrative of violence, disease, and occasionally survival: "Rome is alarmed. Rome is terrified. Rome is sacked. Rome is recovered. Rome is smitten with pestilence. Rome is burned. Rome is rebuilt." Schoemperlen's penchant for literary experimentation is analogous to the methods behind musical remixes or mashups. *By the Book* is one of a growing number of useful templates for how narrative collage can work not only as an aesthetic practice, but also as a new way of understanding and representing human experience.

100 Skills You'll Need for the End of the World (As We Know It)

Nonfiction by Ana Maria Spagna, illust. by Brian Cronin

STOREY PUBLISHING, 2015; ISBN: 978-1612124568; $14.95; 224 PP.
REVIEWED BY REBECCA BAUMANN

QUIRKY, CONCISE, AND artfully depicted, Ana Maria Spagna's one-page shorts in *100 Skills You'll Need for the End of the World (As We Know It)* are much more than prep-advice for Earth's final day. This on-the-go pocket book covers the essentials to the eccentric, all of it crucial for a post-apocalyptic world trying to get back on its feet.

The opening pages contain the basics of societal repair, including Animal Husbandry, Foraging, Shelter Building, Basic First Aid, and a plethora of nifty charts and pictorials with how-to's on reading animal tracks, tying knots, identifying medicinal herbs, and navigating by starlight.

But when the labor and chores are done, what will humans need to stay, well, human? Spagna's witty tutorials on the necessary skills to live past doomsday also account for one innate and deeply personal need: to create, nurture, and share the arts. After the homes are built, crops are thriving, and that pesky dental health is finally under control (yes, toothbrushing is forever), what then, will humans do to uphold creative, social, and psychological health? Spagna outlines it beautifully, giving us the chance to open new artistic breadths through such topics as Daydreaming, Laughing, Music Making, and Storytelling. We even learn about the timelessness of simply Porch Sitting:

> "You can sit on the porch anytime, but late afternoon is best, near sunset on a summer day. Bring something to read, or not, because reading is about thinking and porch sitting is about not thinking. Porch sitting is about not doing anything except noticing the way the light filters through the cottonwoods or how raindrops bounce off the dusty earth."
>
> —69. Porch Sitting

Accompanied by 100 storybook-style illustrations by Brian Cronin for every skill, these pages move beyond the basics of survival 101. Each piece of advice is intentioned, experienced, and centered in both community and individual wellness, leaving room for the little comforts we might miss in this tragically uncomfortable situation.

COUNTRY OF GHOST

POETRY BY GAYLORD BREWER

RED HEN PRESS, 2015; ISBN: 978-1597093132; $18.95; 120 PP.

REVIEWED BY T.M. LAWSON

GAYLORD BREWER'S *Country of Ghost* is a journey that incorporates life and death within each poem through the character Ghost. Brewer reinvents faith in part-fable, part-allegory, and part-magic realism, following Ghost as Ghost (which is only a "you" stuck in perpetual self-reflection) becomes self-aware, testing and confronting the limits of Ghost's existence.

Physical sensation is vital to Brewer's translation of a post-flesh body's needs and desires. Ghost's corporeal appetite, reactions to heat (which, within itself, is a running theme of connected images of fire and burning), and real memories of love and regret hold weight throughout each interaction. Brewer uses the landscape as another motif. His own personal travels serve as a charming backdrop for Ghost to move through and against; "country" is not bordered or static, and becomes as fluid as the character it follows. Ghost goes from the Coves Salnitre in Spain to his wedding day to the "road to Cortavant," encountering memory, imagination (other spirits and psychic phenomena), and religion.

One easily gets the sense of being led through a garden. The poet transforms Catholicism into a malleable playground, featuring the Virgin, Father, and Jesus Christ as playmates. Ghost confronts and lives more fully than the character's previous physical version; in fact, Brewer makes a convincing case that physicality is the true limitation and that death produces an afterlife that resolves lingering earthly concerns. *Country of Ghost* fleshes this sentiment out without dipping into melancholy or a drought of emotion, retaining the vibrancy of language and patterning it across the collection.

> On your back,
>
> you're more buoyant than you were alive,
> arms extended, toes toward sudden sun,
> dragonflies to investigate the corpse.

CONTRIBUTOR NOTES

Allison Adair's poems appear or are forthcoming in *Best New Poets 2015*, *Boston Review*, *Mid-American Review*, *Missouri Review*, *Tahoma Literary Review*, *Tinderbox Poetry Journal*, *The Journal of Compressed Creative Arts*, *Boston Globe*, and the anthology *Hacks*; hypertext projects appear on *The Rumpus* and *Electric Literature*. Winner of the 2014 Fineline Competition, Adair is on the English faculty at Boston College and teaches poetry workshops at Grub Street.

Daniel Aristi was born in Spain. He studied French Literature. He now lives in Switzerland with his wife and two children. Daniel's work has been recently featured or is forthcoming in *Fiction Southeast*, *Puerto del Sol* and *The Conium Review*.

A Southern California native, **Rebecca Baumann** is the Assistant Managing Editor of *The Los Angeles Review* and Outreach Coordinator at Red Hen Press, where she creates grants for the press's funding initiatives and manages the Writing in the Schools program. Outside of the press, she mentors low-performance composition students and assists in teaching English writing labs at Pasadena City College. Rebecca holds an MFA in creative writing through Mount Saint Mary's University.

LAR's nonfiction editor **Ann Beman** has been writing a book about thumbs forever. Her work has appeared in *DIAGRAM*, *The Mojave River Review*, *Bombay Gin*, and *Canoe Journal*, among others. She lives in California's Sierra Nevada with her husband, a chihuahua, and two whatchamaterriers in Kernville, on the Kern River, in Kern County (cue the banjoes).

Alyse Bensel is the author *Not of Their Own Making* (Dancing Girl Press, 2014) and *Shift* (Plan B Press, 2012). Her poetry has most recently appeared in *Mid-American Review*, *Men-*

acing Hedge, *Heavy Feather Review*, and *burntdistrict*, among others. She serves as the Book Reviews Editor at *The Los Angeles Review* and Managing Editor of *Beecher's*.

Michael Chaney has been published in *Michigan Quarterly Review*, *Wigleaf*, and *Epiphany* and has work forthcoming from *Fourth Genre*, *Fourteen Hills*, and *Diagram*. He lives in Vermont and teaches at Dartmouth College.

Adrienne Christian is the author of *12023 Woodmont Avenue* (Willow Books, 2013), coming-of-age poems. She is a Cave Canem fellow, whose work has been featured in *frogpond*, *New Criterion*, *Obsidian*, and others. She earned her Bachelor of Arts in English from the University of Michigan, and her Master of Fine Arts in Creative Writing from Pacific University. Adrienne splits her time between New York City and Oro Valley, Arizona. When she isn't writing, she's entertaining, or traveling to photograph nature.

Allison Coffelt lives and writes in Columbia, Missouri. Her work has appeared or is forthcoming in *Hippocampus*, *Oxford Public Health Magazine*, *Crab Orchard Review*, *museum of americana*, *Prick of the Spindle*, and the Higgs Weldon humor website. She is the winner of the 2015 University of Missouri Essay Prize and finalist in the 2015 *Crab Orchard Review* John Guyon Literary Nonfiction Prize and the 2016 San Miguel Writer's Workshop Essay Contest. She works for the True/False, a nonfiction film festival.

Dante Di Stefano's poetry and essays have appeared recently in *The Writer's Chronicle*, *Shenandoah*, *Brilliant Corners*, *The Southern California Review*, and elsewhere. He was the winner of the Thayer Fellowship in the Arts, the Allen Ginsberg Poetry Award, The Ruth Stone Poetry Prize, The Phyllis Smart-Young Prize in Poetry, The Bea González Prize in Poetry, and an Academy of American Poets College Prize.

José Hernández Díaz is an MFA student at Antioch University Los Angeles. He earned a BA in English from UC Berkeley. His work has appeared in *Best American Nonrequired Reading*, *The Progressive*, *Lumina*, *Witness*, *Huizache*, *Juked*, *Hobart*, *Whiskey Island*, and others. He has served as an editor for *Lunch Ticket* and Floricanto Press.

Stephanie Dickinson lives in New York City. Her novel *Half Girl* and novella *Lust Series* are published by Spuyten Duyvil, as is her recent novel *Love Highway*, based on the 2006 Jennifer Moore murder. Her other books are *Corn Goddess*, *Road of Five Churches*, and *Port Authority Orchids*.

Beth Ann Fennelly directs the MFA Program at the University of Mississippi, where she was named Outstanding Teacher of the Year. She's won grants from the NEA, the MS Arts Commission, and United States Artists. Fennelly has published three full-length poetry books. Her first, *Open House*, won The 2001 Kenyon Review Prize and the Great Lakes College Association New Writers Award, and was a Book Sense Top Ten Poetry Pick. Her second book, *Tender Hooks*, and her third, *Unmentionables*, were published by W. W. Norton & Co. in 2004 and 2008. She has also published a book of nonfiction, *Great with Child*, in 2006, with Norton. Her most recent book is *The Tilted World*, a novel she co-authored with her husband, Tom Franklin. They live in Oxford with their three children.

Melody S. Gee is the author of *Each Crumbling House* (Perugia Press, 2010) and *The Dead in Daylight* (Cooper Dillon Books, 2016). She teaches developmental writing at St. Louis Community College, and lives with her husband and daughters in Missouri. Find her at www.melodygee.com.

Tanya Grae lives and teaches in Florida. She holds an MFA from Bennington and an EdS from Stetson University. Her poems have appeared in *The Florida Review, New South, The Adroit Journal, Sugar House Review*, and other journals.

Peter Grandbois is the author of seven previous books. His work has been shortlisted for both *Best American Essays* and the Pushcart Prize. His plays have been performed in St. Louis, Columbus, Los Angeles, and New York. He is senior editor at *Boulevard* and teaches at Denison University.

Stephanie Barbé Hammer has published short fiction, nonfiction and poetry in *The Bellevue Literary Review, CRATE, Pearl, East Jasmine Review, Apeiron,* and the *Hayden's Ferry Review* among other places. She is the author of *Sex with Buildings (*Dancing Girl Press, 2012), *How Formal?* (Spout Hill Press, 2014), and *The Puppet Turners of Narrow Interior* (Urban Farmhouse Press, 2015). An almost completely recovered career academic, Stephanie teaches at conferences and writers associations and divides her time between Coupeville and Los Angeles with her husband Larry Behrendt. She is a four-time nominee for the Pushcart Prize.

B.J. Hollars is the author of several books, most recently *Dispatches From The Drownings*. He also has two forthcoming in 2015: *From the Mouths of Dogs: What Our Pets Teach Us About Life, Death, and Being Human*, as well as a collection of essays, *This Is Only A Test*. He serves as the reviews editor for *Pleiades*, a mentor for *Creative Nonfiction*, and a professor at the University of Wisconsin-Eau Claire.

Charles Hood is a Research Fellow with Center for Art & Environment at the Nevada Museum of Art, and teaches at Antelope Valley College. Recent work has appeared in *New England Review*, *Catamaran*, *Chautauqua*, and *Diagram*; his book *South x South* won the Hollis Summers Prize, Ohio University Press.

M. Ann Hull's work has appeared in *32 Poems*, *Barrow Street*, *BOXCAR Poetry Review*, and *Mid-American Review*, among others. She has won the Ed Ochester Award and the Academy of American Poets Prize. A former poetry editor of *Black Warrior Review*, she holds an MFA from the University of Alabama.

Rose Hunter is the author of the poetry books *You As Poetry* (Texture Press), *[four paths]* (Texture Press), and *to the river* (Artistically Declined Press), as well as the chapbook *descansos* (dancing girl press). She is from Australia originally, lived in Toronto for ten years, and is now in Puerto Vallarta, Mexico. More information about her is available at Whoever Brought Me Here Will Have To Take Me Home (http://rosehunterblog.wordpress.com).

Sarah Janczak lives in Austin, TX. Her poems have appeared in or are forthcoming from *Colorado Review*, *Hayden's Ferry Review*, *Fjords*, and *Witness*. You can visit her at www.sarahjanczak.com.

Ingrid Jendrzejewski grew up in southern Indiana and studied creative writing and English literature at the University of Evansville before going on to study physics at the University of Cambridge. In past lives, she has been a researcher, teacher, computer games developer, arts administrator, and pizza delivery person, but she is currently taking some time out of employment to be a mother and to write. Links to her work can be found at www.ingridj.com.

Margot Kahn is the author of *Horses That Buck* (University of Oklahoma Press, 2008), the biography of an old rodeo cowboy. She holds an MFA from Columbia University and is a writer-in-residence with Seattle Arts & Lectures.

T.M. Lawson is a writer and poet in Los Angeles, CA, and is currently exploring narratives in hybrid genres in mixed media. Find more at tmlawson.com.

Jenna Le is the author of *Six Rivers* (NYQ Books, 2011), which was a Small Press Distribution Bestseller. Her poetry, fiction, criticism, and translations have appeared or are forthcoming in *AGNI Online, Bellevue Literary Review, The Best of the Raintown Review, Crab Orchard Review, Massachusetts Review,* and *The Village Voice.* She works as a physician in New York.

Lisa Locascio's writing has appeared in *n+1, The Believer, Bookforum, Tin House Flash Fridays,* and the anthology *California Prose Directory: New Writing from the Golden State.* An excerpt of her novel *Jutland Gothic* received a 2015 Pushcart Prize nomination from the journal *Your Impossible Voice.* Lisa edits the LA and San Francisco editions of *Joyland* and the new ekphrastic collaboration magazine *7x7.*

Kristen Nichols lives in California with her family. She has an MFA in creative writing and a writing pedagogy certificate from Antioch University, LA. She was a judge for the 2015 Flannery O'Connor Award for Short Fiction and is a 2016 Peter Taylor Fellow at the *Kenyon Review* Writer's Workshop.

A former US Army interrogator, **Martin Ott** lives in Los Angeles and is the author of six books of poetry and fiction, including *Underdays* (Sandeen Prize winner, University of Notre Dame Press) and *Interrogations* (Fomite Press). More at www.martinottwriter.com.

Daniel Pecchenino lives in Hollywood and is on the Writing Program faculty at the University of Southern California. He is the Assistant Reviews Editor at *The Los Angeles Review,* and his poetry and criticism have appeared in *Gravel, Two Hawks Quarterly, Borderlands: Texas Poetry Review,* and other publications.

Pedro Ponce is the author of *Dreamland,* a novel that is being published in serial form in the online journal *Transmission* (transmission.satellitepress.org).

Glen Pourciau's first collection of stories, *Invite,* won the 2008 Iowa Short Fiction Award. His second story collection is forthcoming from Four Way Books. His stories have been published by *AGNI* Online, *Antioch Review, Epoch, New England Review, Paris Review,* and other magazines.

Doug Ramspeck is the author of five poetry collections. His most recent book, *Original Bodies* (2014), was selected for the Michael Waters Poetry Prize and is published by Southern

Indiana Review Press. Individual poems have appeared in *The Kenyon Review, The Southern Review,* and *The Georgia Review.* He teaches creative writing and directs the Heath Learning Center at The Ohio State University at Lima.

Michael Schmeltzer is the author of *Elegy/Elk River,* winner of the 2015 Floating Bridge Press Chapbook Award. He earned an MFA from the Rainier Writing Workshop. He helps edit *A River & Sound Review* and has work published in *PANK, Rattle,* and *Mid-American Review,* among others.

Leigh Claire Schmidli grew up along Midwestern plains, but now lives with a view of woods-covered hills—orange in fall, purple in spring. She writes poetry, fiction, and essays, loves to read work with lyrical leanings, and cooks meals with a man who calls her Lucy. Her first published piece—a work of flash fiction—recently came out in *Carve Magazine.*

Sarah Sheesley is a freelance writer and teacher based in Albuquerque, New Mexico. She received an MFA from the University of New Mexico where she also served as Managing Editor for *Blue Mesa Review.* Her work has appeared in *Edible Santa Fe* and *The Rumpus.* www.sarahsheesley.com.

Carrie Shipers's poems have appeared in *Hayden's Ferry Review, New England Review, North American Review, Prairie Schooner, The Southern Review,* and other journals. She is the author of *Ordinary Mourning* (ABZ, 2010), *Cause for Concern* (Able Muse, 2015), *Family Resemblances* (University of New Mexico, forthcoming), and two chapbooks.

Judith Skillman, M.A., is the author of fifteen collections of poetry. Her work has appeared in *J Journal, The Southern Review, Tampa Review, Prairie Schooner, FIELD, The Iowa Review, Poetry,* and other journals. Her awards include a Eric Mathieu King grant from the Academy of American Poets. Currently she works on manuscript review: www.judithskillman.com.

Beth Sutton-Ramspeck teaches nineteenth-century British Literature at the Ohio State University at Lima. She is the author of *Raising the Dust: The Literary Housekeeping of Mary Ward, Sarah Grand, and Charlotte Perkins Gilman* and the editor of *Marcella,* by Mary Ward, and *Herland,* by Charlotte Perkins Gilman.

Jessi Terson's work has previously appeared in *Rosebud Magazine, Cleaver Magazine*, and *Anthem Journal*. Her work will also appear in the next issue of *Mad Hatters' Review*. She graduated from Sarah Lawrence College with an MFA in poetry.

Charles Harper Webb's latest book, *Brain Camp,* was published by the University of Pittsburgh Press in 2015. *A Million MFAs Are Not Enough*, a book of essays on American poetry, is forthcoming from Red Hen Press in 2016. Recipient of grants from the Whiting and Guggenheim foundations, Webb teaches Creative Writing at California State University, Long Beach.

thumbprint
of women's book titles
by Cheryl Sorg

Fourteen Hills

THE SAN FRANCISCO STATE UNIVERSITY REVIEW

POETRY
FICTION NON-FICTION
EXPERIMENTAL
ART
14hills.net

2016 Fineline Competition

for prose poems, short shorts,
and anything in between

$1000 First Prize • Deadline: June 1, 2016

2016 Final Judge: Matt Bell, author of *Scrapper* (Soho 2015), *In the House Upon the Dirt Between the Lake the Woods* (Soho, 2013), and *How They Were Found* (Keyhole, 2010)

500-word limit for each poem or short. $10 entry fee (payable online or by check/money order) for each set of three works. Contest is for previously unpublished work only—if the work has appeared in print or online, in any form or part, or under any title, or has been contracted for such, it is ineligible and will be disqualified. Entry fees are non-refundable. All participants will receive *Mid-American Review* v. XXXVII, no. 1, where the winner will be published. Submissions will not be returned. Manuscripts need not be left anonymous. Contest is open to all writers, except those associated with the judge or *Mid-American Review*, past or present. Judge's decision is final.

submit: marsubmissions.bgsu.edu

Mid-American Review
Department of English
Bowling Green State University
Bowling Green OH 43403
419-372-2725 • mar@bgsu.edu

SEATTLE'S FINEST POETRY, PROSE, ART & PHOTOGRAPHY

PACIFICA

LITERARY REVIEW

ISSUES
FEBRUARY
& JULY

pacificareview.com

Last Train to the Missing Planet
Poetry by Kim Dower
978-1-59709-353-8 / $17.95 / Mar. 29th

Expect the unexpected, while being entertained, engaged, inspired: experience the always present but rarely recognized miraculous moments of our everyday lives in this anticipated third collection from Kim Dower.

Praise for *Last Train to the Missing Planet*:

"What a pleasure it is to settle into Kim Dower's latest collection. Dower's poetry creates a quiet space around itself, full of worldly, humorous insights into life as it is."

—Janet Fitch

"These poems speak in the voice of an old, trusted friend who knows you, who has come to visit and remind you of who you are and what a life is all about. They speak not of the highs and lows, but about the grey space between tragedy and tenderness, memory and loss, fragility and perseverance—that space where the soul and the truest self live."

—Richard Blanco, Presidential Inaugural Poet

Vampire Planet
Poetry by Ron Koertge
978-1-59709-760-4 / $17.95 / Apr. 1st

Vampire Planet is an eclectic, witty, and often moving New & Selected collection of poems from a writer whom former US Poet Laureate Billy Collins calls "the wisest, most entertaining wise guy in American poetry." Jim Knipfel, hailed by Thomas Pynchon as "a born storyteller," presents a darkly comic, Midwestern gothic portrayal of America's Dairyland.

Praise for *Vampire Planet*:

"Is anyone writing poems that are as memorable, masterful, and quirky as Ron Koertge's? If you want the lowdown on Lilith, and if you can bear to read about Lois Lane aging, and if you long to know the unsavory truth about Lazarus after he returned from the dead, this deliciously smart and entertaining collection of poems is the one you've been looking for!"

—Steve Kowit

"Wit, the impeccably dressed and better educated sibling of funny, suffers an unstable reputation: clever yet aloof, socially polished but oddly cold. In the warmer, less formal surroundings of Ron Koertge's poems, however, wit lets down its guard and, behold: charm, intelligence, amazing inventiveness, and a kind of sweetness in its patient regard for a world so frequently bereft of those qualities. So what could be more welcome than a new Koertge collection, where wit presides, and wisdom elegantly clothed in laughter is always in attendance."

—B.H. Fairchild

Available from the Chicago Distribution Center
To place an order: (800) 621-2736 / www.redhen.org

SAVE THE DATE   OCTOBER 30, 2016

RED HEN PRESS

22ᴺᴰ BENEFIT CHAMPAGNE LUNCHEON
RITA DOVE, ALAN LIGHTMAN, JILL BIALOSKY

11 AM *at* THE WESTIN PASADENA
191 NORTH LOS ROBLES AVENUE, PASADENA, CA

www.redhen.org/events/benefit
🐦 benefit@redhen.org

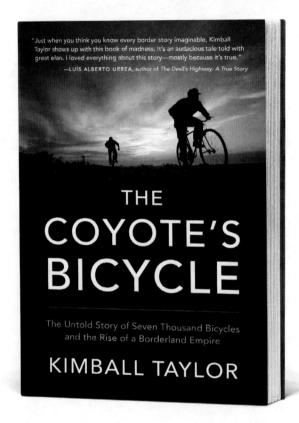